# Foods
# of the Early
# American West

# Mike Moore

Historical Enterprises, LLC
Gallatin, TN

Cover:
*Last Light* by Joe Velazquez
http://www.joevelazquez.com

Published by:
Historical Enterprises, LLC
PO Box 1316
Gallatin, TN 37066
615-230-9853
http://www.historicalenterprises.com

Copyright © 2014
Mike Moore

ISBN: 0-9722308-7-4

*To all my friends who I have shared a fire and a meal with: the twenty-five plus years of eating together has taught us all a lot.*

*B*ut stay –
behold the Dinner Table,
*a table cloth of Dimmest sable,*
*no other than a Buffalo robe*
*spread on the earth a table good,*
*covered with cups & plates & tin to hold our*
    *meat & coffee in.*
*And there's fat Bacon fried in fat, and Hoe cake*
    *– What do you think of that!*
*Believe hoe cake could smell so good?*

**Matthew Field**

# Preface

*Instead of the many apologies generally offered to the public by an author who has the hardihood to present them what, in spite of all prefaces, it will either accept or refuse, I take the liberty to explain at once to the reader with what intention I undertook my excursion, and under what circumstances I pursued it; and he will accordingly be enabled to perceive if the records of such a journey may suit his needs or not.*
Dr. Fredrick Wislizenus

# Introduction

So much of our western American history has to do with tactile items like guns, equipment, and clothes. But when we use only these to show how people lived at that time and what our history was like, we overlook some very basic elements of their lives. I hope this book not only broadens your knowledge on a vital part of the average western traveler's everyday life, but helps keep you well fed too. It always surprises me to see the amount of information available, when you look for it. Food, in all shapes and forms, was thought of, written about and commented on by individuals in the early west for us later readers to see.

This book was not meant to include recipes, for we don't see them used in the original journals or diaries; but to show the wide variety of foods that the individuals in the early west ate.

When looking in the journals, diaries and autobiographies in my western history library, I find that one thing is mentioned at each camp and fills more pages than any other item: food. The foods of the Fur Trade are a varied lot, with some much more appetizing than others, as you will see. But, as no one I know of has taken the subject at hand and bound the information in a single volume, here is my contribution on the topic. We only see the actual foods found at this time in the original journals, diaries or autobiographies, since other forms of books (biographical, narrative, etc.) do not give the specifics that are found in primary records. This is one of the many reasons first-person information is always best.

The Fur Trade was a place where people came together and shared the same dinner "table." The edibles they consumed can be easily divided into groups and subgroups: what was traded at the forts and posts, what could be purchased at rendezvous, what they could find for themselves, and what they learned to eat from others. I hope these pages add to your knowledge about the early west and also help to make your camps more interesting and you well fed.

Mike Moore

*Hunger is said to be a capital sauce, and if so
our meal was well seasoned, for we had been living
for some days on boiled corn alone, and had the
grace to thank heaven for meat of any quality.*
Warren Angus Ferris

# Table of Contents

# An Active Frontier Life Required Fuel

**P**ROVIDING daily provisions was a priority for anyone in the early American west. It took a lot of energy to be in the elements all day in every season, to travel and to live. These men had mainly a meat diet, with seasonal fruit and berries, a spattering of breads or bread substitutes along with some purchased items for however long they lasted.

Their terms and expressions for food maybe different than ours, but the thoughts are the same as we have. They needed to eat to keep up their energy and enjoyed cooking and eating all types of food.

Most individuals in the west were lean in body. Why? Because they had lots of exercise, a lean diet and different eating schedules than we have. Most of the recorded journal entries show only two times of sitting down to eat per day, whether in the forts or on the trail. The ones who were portly are noted and stand out in a crowd (this is true for all races and ethnic backgrounds).

## Foods of the Early American West

*No breakfast, feel very much purified in the flesh...*

Nathaniel Wyeth (1)

Most foods consumed at other times of the day were very functional, such as dried meat and water, usually eaten on the trail while riding. A day's routine was probably a quick, light breakfast; a lunch, which was a little less while in the saddle or sitting on a wagon's bench, and dinner being

the main meal of the day.

Food does seem to taste better in the mountains over a camp fire, and for those whose diet varied from too much at a sitting when there was plenty, to hardly any or none at all during days of travel, food in all of its facets was written about. And anything that changed their diet or added to this was noted, since most of the edibles were plain and constantly the same. Complicated dishes were the exception for all races; more common were simple dishes of soups and stews or one item meals. This was why exceptional dinners and celebrations were written about in journals and the diaries.

These men put travel and their occupation in first priority. They did not have the luxury of spending all day cooking, so easy regional and ethnic foods were typically the main course of the day.

1.    Nathaniel Wyeth, *The Journals of Captain Nathaniel J. Wyeth's Expeditions to the Oregon Country, 1831-1836*, Ye Galleon Press, Fairfield, 1997, page 79.

# *Foodstuffs to Get Them Along the Way*

*"...a little tea, rice, fruits, crackers, etc., suffice very well for the first fortnight..."*

Josiah Gregg (1)

**F**OOD items were purchased at a mercantile store, trading posts and ordered in from various coasts to help the men get a good start on their trips west. But these foodstuffs did not last long and also spoiled easily. Because of this, basics like sugar, flour, tea and coffee were soon gone – and then done without. Besides, the experienced guides recommended bringing just enough food to keep hardy travelers from starving until they reached an imaginary line that was where the western game animals could be seen and harvested. This was usually the start of the buffalo hunting land. This undefined area varied year to year, depending on hunting pressure, weather and man's changing of the frontier.

# Foods of the Early American West

*Our fare consisted of bacon and hard-tack – no sugar, nor coffee – for three or four days, after which we each received a small piece of sheep meat, as we had a drove to last us until we got into the buffalo.*

Charles Larpenteur (2)

The western guide books of that day also gave their recommendations on how much food was needed for each person for such a trip west. Common fare for this first section of the trip was bacon, flour, coffee, beans and beef. They supplemented all this with fish they caught and any fresh fruit they came upon while heading west, since springtime was when most caravans started westward. We will discuss each of these in depth in later chapters.

Sometimes, the food supply brought with them did not last or spoiled before this imaginary line was crossed. River crossings, morning dews, poor quality staples and sometimes, just hearty appetites made the supplies lighten with each day traveled. The following journal entries will give you how well a few of the western groups ate before reaching buffalo country:

*Old Provost, being conducteur, was in our mess which was an excellent one. We generally had a large bowl of capital soup, meat roasted & boiled, generally some game, plenty of potatoes and onions, biscuits and & c. and plenty of tea and coffee.*

William Fairholme (3)

*...we take with us for the first week some provisions, such as ham, ship-biscuit, tea and coffee. Afterwards, we depend on hunting.*

Fredrick Wislizenus (4)

Another good example of what they carried with them is shown by George Sibley's journal. He made the following chart as part of the official government record, before he left to survey the Santa Fe Trail: (5)

**The wagons loaded as follows:**

| | |
|---|---|
| 2 bags of rice – 76 lbs each | 152 lbs |
| 5 bags of flour – in all | 614 lbs |
| 2 bags of corn meal | 300 lbs |
| 1 bag of salt | 60 lbs |
| 1 keg of whiskey | [no weight listed] |
| 1 box of bacon | 400 lbs |

Captain Randolph Marcy's emigrant book, *The Prairie Traveler*, (6) is a little late for our time frame, but his seven pages on provisions and how to prepare for the western trip is quite interesting. Marcy's comments on dried vegetables, how to preserve bacon (he recommended packing it surrounded by bran), double packing flour in stout canvas bags that were securely sewn shut and the use of pemmican still fits well here. A few advances had been discovered by the 1850's and some of them, like canned vegetables, soldering up of skimmed butter containers, sugar to be put in Indian rubber or gutta-percha packs, preserved potatoes and the first comments I have seen on citric acid as a antidote to scurvy are described in his guide book.

Lansford Hasting's *The Emigrant Guide* also comments on this important initial aspect of provisions:

> *Then it would seem that, although the buffalo are vastly numerous, they cannot be relied upon; yet to avoid encumbering himself with the very large quantities of meat which his family would require, the emigrant can drive cattle, which will afford him a very good substitute, not only for the beef of the buffalo, but for bacon, and what is more important, is that they can be relied upon, under all circumstances.* (7)

All these preparations were an important part of a successful trip. When Joseph Nicollet found open boxes of supplies when starting to pack before leaving, he was angry at the shippers who had not only charged him for hauling the goods, but unbeknown to him also took a percentage of the goods:

> *On my arrival here, James informed me that two boxes had been opened on the journey from St. Peters here by the men who brought the train containing your boxes of merchandise and provisions. We proceeded to verify the statement, and now we find that one of the boxes containing 90 lbs of sugar, brought from St. Louis, had been reduced to two-thirds, and one of the two boxes containing Pittsburgh biscuits had been reduced to one-sixth...* (8)

Stephen Long's list of provisions for his 1819 western trip included:
500 lbs of pork
3 bushels of parched corn
5 gallons of whiskey
25 lbs of coffee
30 lbs of sugar,
a small quantity of salt...

Stephen Long (9)

These few pages have given you an idea on the food provisions western travelers started out with. Many today do not think of the start of the trip's food since the romance and adventure of getting their own meat, free

**17**

but for the cost of lead and powder, are usually all we ever think of. Yet, a good start in this often unrecognized area gave the whole trip a greater chance of success.

1. Josiah Gregg, *Commerce of the Prairies,* Milo Milton Quaife editor, University of Nebraska Press, Lincoln, 1967, pages 21-22.
2. Charles Larpenteur, *Forty Years a Fur Trader,* University of Nebraska Press, 1989, page 18.
3. William Fairholme, *Journal of an Expedition to the Grand Prairies of the Missouri,* Arthur Clark, Spokane, 1996, 1840, page 79.
4. Dr. Fredrick Wislizenus, *A Journey to the Rocky Mountains in the Year 1839,* Ye Galleon Press, Fairfield, 1989, page 30.
5. Kate Gregg, *Road to Santa Fe,* (Sibley's journal) University of New Mexico Press, Albuquerque, 1968, page 176.
6. Captain Randolph Marcy, *The Prairie Traveler,* Applewood Books, Bedford, 1993, pages 30-7.
7. Lansford Hasting, *The Emigrant's Guide,* Applewood books, Bedford, no date, page 144.
8. Joseph Nicollet, *Joseph N. Nicollet on the Plains and Prairies,* Minnesota Historical Society, St. Paul, 1993, page 225.
9. Stephen Long, *From Pittsburg to the Rocky Mountains,* Maxine Benson, Fulcrum, Golden, 1988, page 149.

# A Multitude of Influences

**T**HE foods which show up on the western American frontier include influences from the Scotch-Irish, English, French, Native American and Hispanic cultures. While the average American cuisine was available all year round back where they started from, most of what these individuals ate went through cycles in the west. Meat was the mainstay of all their diets throughout the year but its quality varied with the different months of the year (fall was best; late winter worst), vegetables and natural growing fruits only had a few weeks of maturity at certain periods of the year (some in spring, others in fall); so much of the daily food had to be acquired from different avenues.

A feast-and-famine routine was experienced by the individuals who lived during this time and is shown repeatedly in the early journals. Keeping a few weeks' foods on hand did not happen all the time as there was no good way of preserving food, except by drying and smoking. And you will see that many groups ate as much as they could when what they had was fresh during the warm periods of the year. Monotony in their diet was also a common item they wrote about, as the advancing people only knew a certain amount of variety to be available in each region at a specific time. So, when we see any type of unique food or meal, it was commented on because it was special.

Individuals had their own foods they were used to and comfortable with. These were mostly the regional foods they grew up with or consumed as adults. When their diets changed because of entering a different regional or cultural area, the physical effects were noted, usually very discretely.

*My comrades had told me that we should now get a sickness called by them* le mal de vache; *it is a dysentery caused by eating too much fat meat alone, and some have died from it.*

Charles Larpenteur (1)

When viewing the different foods shown in this book, always think where and when the passage was written, how far they were from getting their original supplies, what was easily available to them, how they were eating it, if it was naturally (and cheaply) found or if it was something that could be traded or purchased. Recognizing these things will help mentally clear up the order, uniqueness and appearance of all foods.

Early into trips west, individuals had much more "civilized" foods. As they progressed down the trails, they found themselves in the middle of the country where diets changed along with the scenery. This is where we see the different regional fares really show up. Many kinds of marine foodstuffs are seen in journals written in the northwest coast, and buffalo on the central plains. Fowl and small game were noted in the southwest, and common in all regions. You will see individual chapters in this book on the foods of the major ethnic groups, Hispanic and Native American. When you recognize the foods written about, it would be a likely – and truthful – response to think, "We still have many of these in our everyday diet."

So, let's see what the primary sources say about the largest and most common food group – meat.

1.   Charles Larpenteur, *Forty Years a Fur Trader on the Upper Missouri*, University of Nebraska Press, Lincoln, 1989, page 22.

# *Meats*

*Our bacon box is running low,*
*And we are out of buffalo,*
*And Walnut Creek is running high*
*And the wagons can't get over dry.*
*And hints are heard of short allowance*
*Unless we kill a Bull or Cow hence.*
*So mounted soon, our way we take…*

Matthew Field (1)

THE most common item seen in all the descriptions of food was meat. This food, in all its forms – whether deer, elk, buffalo, sheep, beef or any of the other smaller animals – made up a very large percentage of what was eaten daily, all through the calendar year. Both David Meriwether and Dr. Fredrick Wislizenus commented on this kind of meat diet:

*We had passed nearly six months in the wilderness. In that time we had covered under daily hardships about three thousand miles, had slept on the bare ground in all kinds of weather, and had lived almost exclusively on meat. Nevertheless, we all fairly overflowed with health…*

David Meriwether (2)

*Considering the absence of bread, and the traveler's life in the open air and daily exercise, it is not remarkable that the appetite makes unusual demands, and people, who frequently were accustomed to eat scarcely a pound of meat daily, can consume eight and ten times as much of fresh buffalo meat, without being gluttons on that account.*

Dr. Fredrick Wislizenus (3)

*White Cloud and myself rarely ever returned to camp without a deer, and it was astonishing how much meat we could eat when we had neither bread or vegetables. Indeed, it required a large deer to supply our supper and our breakfast next morning…*

David Meriwether (4)

This may seem so strange to us today, for we don't consider a one item meal as complete. Our meals include the three main food groups with side dishes and desserts. This way of thinking was not the mindset of the mid-1800's individual. You ate what was available and sometimes a lot of it. As a friend said to Charles Larpenteur when food was plenty:

*"Back up your cart, Larpenteur, for another load."* (5)

E. Willard Smith also comments on how much buffalo meat a man could eat without injury:

*To-day we came across several large herds of Buffalo, and the hunters succeeded in getting some very good meat, which was quite an agreeable change. We all ate voraciously of it. It would astonish the inhabitants of the city to drop in upon us at some of our meals, after we had been on short allowances for two or three days. It is incredible what a large quantity of Buffalo-meat a man can eat without injury.* (6)

Buffalo was eaten by itself for many meals, if that was all that was available. Buffalo was to many **the** meat of the west, not only for the adventure of acquiring it, but for its texture, taste, simplicity in cooking and the multiple flavors within the animal's sections.

*…no other kind of meat can compare with that of the female bison, in good condition. With it we require no seasoning; we boil, roast, or fry it, as we please, and live*

*upon it solely, without bread or vegetables of any kind, and what seems most singular, we never tire of or disrelish it, which would be the case with almost any other meat, after living upon it exclusively for a few days.*

Warren Ferris (7)

Sir Charles Murray, an English world traveler who spent a summer living with the Pawnee in 1835, had this to say about meat as a food source:

*"But I was no longer a civilized man – hunger had triumphed over the last traces of civilization, - I received with thankfulness, and ate with eagerness, a good piece of the warm liver untouched by fire, water or salt, and I found it agreeable to the palate and as tender as any morsel I ever tasted." (8)*

He described it as *"extremely delicate food"* (9) and especially liked the ribs, tongue, hump and liver. (10) Even the refined Susan Magoffin liked soups made of hump ribs, and described how her traveling group also dried the meat on stretched ropes. (11)

So, let's give a few other references on Buffalo as a food source:

*After our mules were unpacked and our baggage was arranged, a kettle of boiled buffalo tongues was brought in; a strong cup of coffee was made from our stores, and we took supper alongside a good fire, after which symptoms of good humor returned.*

Charles Larpenteur (12)

*Buffalo meat tastes better much better than beef. The meat of the cows is usually tenderer and fatter than that of the bulls, and particularly deserves the preference in the summer, when the bulls are lean and unpalatable. From the slain buffalo, only the best pieces are taken, namely the tongue, the ribs, the hump ribs, the meat on the either side of the backbone and the marrow bones, with at times the liver and kidney... the thigh bones are thrown into the fire until roasted, and then cracked open, yielding the finest marrow that ever tickled a gourmand's palate.*

Dr. Fredrick Wislizenus (13)

*The flesh of the cow buffalo is considered far superior to that of the domestic beef and it is so impregnated with salt that it requires but little seasoning when cooked.*

Osborne Russell (14)

Everyone comments on how much the tribes relied on the buffalo, but it seems that the whites of the day came a close second. Stephen Long talked of cooking a buffalo hump *"Indian Style"* in his journal – which he described

23

as having the hair burned off and burying the meat in a hole about a foot deep which, heated by a strong fire over it. He declared it to be excellent food when cooked like this. (15)

Smaller sections of a buffalo's meat were cut up to be used. The most popular and labor intensive way to see this was in its use in a sausage or *boudin* (a French word meaning *stuffed*). Cleaned and turned inside out intestines had small pieces of meat and fat stuffed into it.

*Meanwhile, divers of the company had joined the butcher, and, while some were greedily feeding upon liver and gall, others helped themselves to marrow-bones, "boudins," and intestinum medulæ, (choice selections with mountaineers) and others, laden with rich spoils, hastened their return to commence the more agreeable task of cooking and eating…This "depouille" (fleece fat) was full two inches upon the animals back, and the other dainties were enough to charm the eyes and excite the voracity of an epicure. The camp soon presented a busy and amusing spectacle. Each one was ornamented with delicious roasts, "en appolas," on sticks planted aslope around it, attentively watched by the longing voyageurs, who awaited the slow process of cooking. Some were seen with thin slices from the larder, barely heated through by the agency of a few coals, retreating from the admiring throng to enjoy solo their half-cooked morsels, -- others, paring off bit by bit from the fresh-turned hissing roasts, while their opposite received the finishing operation of the fire – and others, tossing their everted "boudins" into the flames, and in a few seconds withdrawing for the repast, each seizing his ample share, bemouthed the end in quick succession to sever the chosen esculent, which, while yielding to the eager teeth, coursed miniature rivulets of oily*

Getting ready to start the stuffing!

*exuberance from the extremities of the active orifice, bedaubing both face and chin, and leaving its delighted eater in all the glories of grease!*

Rufus Sage (16)

"*Let us have some boudins, boys,*" *said the ever active Smith…muster something to chop up this meat on, before the gut gets hard! … If there is nothing in that country so good as these puddings, neither is there anything more easily cooked. Everyone had a pile of meat cut half the size of a dice; Jim had his in long thin strings, cut with the grain, in the Indian fashion. The other heaps were put together and crammed into the gut as it was turned inside out and tied with a whang at regular  intervals. So that, when cut into portions, it should not lose the juice. This was set up to boil…*

Sir William Drummond Stewart (17)

Other sections of the buffalo were also enjoyed:

*It is equally amusing to me, and rather disgusting withal, to see the "Old birds" as they call themselves, dispose of the only liver brought into camp. Instead of boiling, frying or roasting it, they laid hold of it raw, and, sopping it, mouthful by mouthful in gall, swallowed it with surprising gusto.*

Rufus Sage (18)

*He cut the ribs along their root, thus opening a door to get at the pudding gut – the same as that used in the red deer in Scotland, but in the case of the bison, it is stuffed with the meat inside the loin cut small and is considered the greatest luxury in mountain cooking.*

William Drummond Stewart (19)

*After an hour's dumb conversation, a dish of roasted Buffaloe tongues*

A successful hunt.

*was set before me…*

Osborne Russell (20)

We also see that the men liked cow (the female buffalo) meat better than the male or bull, which why the old saying shows up – *"better fat cow, than poor bull,"* since the bulls were tougher to eat. Also during the late winter months of January, February and March; the animals lost whatever small amount of fat they had and were shrunken in size. Since the grass the buffalo ate was dead, dry and covered with snow, in the cold they used up more energy getting the food they required which made them lose weight and become lean.

*The meat of the cow is infinitely preferable to that of the male buffalo; but that of the bull, particularly if killed in the mountains, is in better condition during the winter months. From the end of June to September bull-meat is rank and tough, and almost uneatable; while the cows are in perfection, and as fat as stall-fed oxen, the depouille, or fleece, exhibiting frequently four inches and more of solid fat.*

George Ruxton (21)

It makes sense that buffalo was the largest percentage of meat hunted, for one well-placed shot could bring down an animal that would feed a number of families for a few days with a very low expense in arrows, powder and lead, or any other way of procuring a meal.

Like today, buffalo meat was usually cooked only to about one level less than we would usually like our meat cooked. If this was not done, the buffalo meat (of whatever part or section of the animal) would end up dry and lose some of its taste.

Other species of animals were hunted in different regions:

*Sheep Elk Deer Buffaloe and Bear Skins mostly supply the Mountaineers with clothing bedding and lodges while the meat of the same animals supplies them with food.*

Osborne Russell (22)

Osborne Russell had a unique fondness for Big Horn Sheep, writing, *its flesh has a similar taste to Mutton but its flavor is more agreeable and the meat more juicy...* (23)

His journal gives a number of entries that shows how he found the animal and its food worth the danger in its hunting and considered it to be *"rich provisions."* (24)

*The Sheep were all very fat so that this could be called no other than high living both as regarded altitude of position and rich provisions.*

Osborne Russell (25)

He and his group stayed hunting these animals until the deep snow came: *We lived on fat mutton until the snow drove us from the Mountain in Feby.* (26) Russell later came to his senses and finally swore off hunting them after recalling some of the dangerous things he had done to get within shooting range.

We know of others who also liked and hunted Big Horn Sheep. Jedediah Smith records in his journal that he *killed a M[ountain]t sheep.*

*The game, par excellence of the Rocky Mountains and that which takes precedence in a comestible point of view, is the carnero cimmaron of the Mexicans, the Bighorn or Mountain sheep...*

George Ruxton (27)

Venison (deer) was a common source of food:

*Mr Richardson killed a fawn so we have 2 meals ahead besides two night's supper.*

Nathaniel Wyeth (28)

*My hunting was confined principally to black tailed deer.*

Rufus Sage (29)

Elk is another western animal found in the journals:

*Here we encamped on a small clear spot and killed the fattest elk I ever saw. It was a large buck, the fat on his rump measured seven inches thick, he had 14 spikes of branches on the left horn and 12 on the right.*

Osborne Russell (30)

*A large fire was soon blazing encircled with sides of Elk ribs and meat cut in slices supported on sticks down which the grease ran in torrents...*

Osborne Russell (31)

But elk was not liked by all – George Ruxton thought the animals were strong flavored, more like "poor bull" than venison, gamey in taste and stringy. The texture and color of elk meat is different than any other than I have ever had, yet I enjoy it.

Some animals, like bear, were eaten not only for the meat, but for its fat, which was not abundant in most western animals. Elk, deer, and antelope are all very lean meat. The hump on a buffalo is marbled, which is why it was prized. When you see entries of eating beaver tail, it is because the tail is all gristle and the men's bodies were grease-starved. Most times, the journals do not tell us the difference between black bear and Grizzly, but lump the two together.

*Our Camp Kettles had not been greased for some time: as we were continually boiling thistle roots in them during the day: but now four of them containing about 9 gallons each were soon filled with fat bear meat cut in very small pieces and hung over a fire which all hands were employed in keeping up with the utmost impatience:*

Osborne Russell (32)

Of the pronghorn antelope, Dr. Fredrick Wislizenus tells us: *the meat is rather tender, but lean and dry.* (33) Zebulon Pike calls antelope *cabrie*, and notes in his journal they hunted them a lot.

*In the mean time, our hunters killed two buffalo; the latter, however, is seldom found in this country: though it bounds in black and white tailed deer, elk, sheep, antelopes and sometimes moose, and the white mountain goats have been killed here.*

Warren Ferris (34)

What other kinds of meats are recorded in journals? It might surprise you!

"*Killed a wild hog, which on examination I found to be very different from the tame breed, smaller, brown, long hair and short legs: they are found in all parts between the Red river and the Spanish settlements.*"

Zebulon Pike (35)

*My considerate host set before me a vessel, filled with the choicest morsels of deer and lynx, both fat and tender, of which I partook freely. The flesh of the latter is far superior to the meat of the deer; and is the best I ever tasted, except that of the female bison.*

Warren Ferris (36)

As you can see, meat was a main staple for any group in the early west. It provided protein and was relatively easy to obtain. With the added items harvested from these animals, like the hides, bones, fat, internal organs and miscellaneous smaller objects that were useful, big game animals were number one on the list when it came to hunting for dinner.

1. Matthew Field, *Matt Field on the Santa Fe Trail,* John Sunder, editor, University of Oklahoma Press, Norman, 1995, page 16.
2. Dr. Fredrick Wislizenus, *A Journey to the Rocky Mountains in the Year 1839,* Ye Galleon Press, Fairfield, 1989, page 147.
3. Wislizenus, pages 51-2.
4. David Meriwether, *My Life in the Mountains and on the Plains,* University of Oklahoma Press, Norman, 1965, page 59.
5. Charles Larpenteur, *Forty Years a Fur Trader on the Upper Missouri,* University of Nebraska Press, 1989, pages 126-7.
6. E. Willard Smith, Colorado Historical Society, Colorado Magazine, *With the Fur Traders of Colorado,* July 1950, page 170.
7. Warren Ferris, *Life in the Rocky Mountains,* Old West Publishing, Denver, 1983, page 113-4.
8. Sir Charles Murray, *Travels in North America during the Years 1834, 1835 & 1836, Travels in North America,* William Blackwood and Sons, Edinburgh, 1900, page 223.
9. Murray, page 196.
10. Murray, page 309.
11. Susan Magoffin, *Down the Santa Fe Trail and into Mexico,* Stella Drumm, editor, Yale University Press, New Haven, 1962, page 43.
12. Larpenteur, page 161.
13. Wislizenus, page 51.
14. Osborne Russell, *Journal of a Trapper,* University of Nebraska Press, Lincoln, 1986, page 139.

15. Maxine Benson, *From Pittsburg to the Rocky Mountains, Major Stephen Long's Expedition 1819-1820,* Fulcrum Books, Golden, Colorado, 1988, page 133.

16. Rufus Sage, *Rocky Mountain Life,* University of Nebraska Press, Lincoln, 1982, page 66.

17. Sir William Drummond Stewart, *Edward Warren*, Mountain Press, Missoula, 1986, page 92.

18. Sage, page 64.

19. Stewart, page 89.

20. Russell, page 37.

21. George Frederick Ruxton, *Ruxton of the Rockies, page 249.*

22. Russell, page 58.

23. Russell, page 134.

24. Russell, page 25.

25. Russell, page 25.

26. Russell, pages 93 – 95.

27. Ruxton, page 149.

28. Nathaniel J. Wyeth, *The Journals of Captain Nathaniel J. Wyeth's Expeditions to the Oregon Country, 1831-1836,* Ye Galleon Press, Fairfield, 1997, page 94.

29. Sage, page 345.

30. Russell, page 29.

31. Russell, page 63.

32. Wislizenus, page 39.

33. Ferris, page 233.

34. Russell, page 9.

35. Pike, page 231.

36. Ferris, page 318.

## Fishing

*25th. Finished crossing at 10 o'clock; a good supply of fish caught last night and this morning.*

Alphonso Wetmore (1)

**F**ISH is an often overlooked source of food for early western travelers. So many individuals think that bigger is better when classifying the animals that were consumed, but fish do show up, in amazing numbers of entries, as a way to supplement their diets and give them variety. Remember, many of these western white men ate fish in their Eastern and Midwestern homes before coming west. They knew how to easily prepare this food source and which species they preferred.

It is interesting to see fish as a trade item, a survival food, a change in the diet and a food that could be preserved. And not all of the fish were seasonal, like the salmon which were only caught in their annual runs. Nathaniel Wyeth, John Townsend, and Zenas Leonard all wrote on fishing with some form of a rod and hook while in the west. Their manner of fishing may not be what we use today, but it is interesting to see the many different ways this animal was caught.

Nathaniel Wyeth's journal tells of catching salmon, trout and catfish. Once he sent three of his men down the creek to fish and they returned with twenty-one salmon and trout. (2) He and his group also traded for fish on different occasions. One time, they gave four fishing hooks for eight fish; each of the fish weighing about four pounds each. (3) In a different trade, the fish he acquired were already split and dried, and they were not fresh. This probably has more to do with the time of the year of the trade and not his interest in how it was preserved.

There is an interesting story in Wyeth's journal where an Indian was suspected of stealing a knife and would not open his robe when he was confronted about it. What they found under his robe when they pushed the search was a case – not holding a gun, but Wyeth's fishing rod. (4) Now, this is good to know, for we see not only crude fishing equipment used at this time, but also that people owned complete rods with cases.

To reinforce Wyeth's writing on use of up-to-date equipment, at least for the 1830's; here are two quotes from John Townsend's narrative where he writes not only about his attempts at fishing, but what he read and kept in mind on this topic:

*Near us flows the clear deep water of the Sisadee...The river, here, contains a great number of large trout, some grayling and a small narrow mouthed white fish, resembling a herring. They are all frequently taken with the hook, and, the trout particularly, afford excellent sport to the lovers of angling. Old Isaac Walton would be in his glory here, and the precautionary measures which he so strongly recommends in approaching a trout stream, he would not have to practice, as the fish is not shy, and bites quickly and eagerly at a grasshopper or minnow. (5)*

*In the afternoon we made camp on Ross' Creek, a small branch of Snake River. The pasture here is better than we have had for two weeks, and the stream contains an abundance of excellent trout. Some of these are enormous and very fine eating. They bite eagerly at a grasshopper or minnow, but the largest are shy, and the sportsman requires to be carefully concealed in order to take them. We have none of the fine tackle, jointed rods, reel, and silkworm gut of the accomplished city sportsman; we have only a piece of common cord, and a hook seized on with half hitches* [because they had no eyes in the hooks], *with a willow rod cut from the banks of the stream; but with this rough equipment we take as many trout as we wish, and who could do more, even with all the curious contrivances of old Isaac Walton or Christopher North?* (6)

Others, like Zenas Leonard and Jedediah Smith, mention fishing in their journals:

*...we still continued to travel subsisting chiefly on mussels and small fish which we caught in the river...*(7)

*...and we caught some pretty good fish with the hook and line.* (8)

*Their mode of taking salmon is a very simple one. The whole tackle consists of a pole about twelve feet long, with a large hook attached to the end. This machine they keep constantly trailing in the water, and when the fish approaches the surface, by a quick and dexterous jerk, to fasten the iron into his side and shake him off in the canoe. They say they take so many fish that it is necessary for them to land about three times a day to deposit them.*

John Townsend (9)

*Here also, Richard caught fresh salmon, which made us another good meal...*
Narcissa Whitman (10)

*...arrived at Jacksons Lake where we concluded to spend the 4th of July, at the outlet. July 4th I caught about 20 very fine salmon trout which together with fat mutton buffaloe beef and coffee and the manner in which it was served up constituted a dinner that ought to be considered independent even by Britons.*
Osborne Russell (11)

*The rivers of Oregon, in the abundance and quality of their fish, are unparalleled....So great is their number they are frequently taken by the hand; and with the aid of a net, several barrels may be caught at a single haul...*
Rufus Sage (12)

Charles Murray, an Englishman on his way to live among the Pawnees wrote while at Fort Leavenworth:

35

*Among other articles for the supply of the table, one of the most abundant to be met with here is the catfish. I found it somewhat coarse, but not unpalatable. These fish are caught of a most enormous size, and in great quantities, by the settlers on the banks of the river, one of whom told me he caught four in the course of one morning weighing above 50 lbs. each.* (13)

Those who did not have the equipment, patience or the time to spend on a bank holding a pole, traded for this foodstuff. Many of the white travelers did this and the stories that go with these activities are worth mentioning here. George Brewerton wanted to trade a few charges of powder for a fish while visiting a band of the Utes. A few minutes later, one of the men from the tribe returned with a fish; Brewerton did not notice until it was on the fire cooking that the fish had an arrow wound in its back.

They were wondering how it got there, when two of their men came into camp carrying as much fish as they could handle. They had found a small icy stream nearby, about knee deep, where the fish were swarming. These men had killed the fish with sticks. The next day the whole camp set out to get more and Brewerton used an old bayonet fastened to a stick to get his. They harvested five dozen that day – along with Brewerton's twinge of rheumatism which stayed with him long after. (14)

*Two or 3 dozen of fine catfish was caught & in fact all the tributaries of the Kanzas seem well stocked with that species of fish and have been easily taken when ever the water has been low enough to permit us to approach the main Banks of the streams...*

James Clyman (15)

*This morning, I sent 5 men down the creek fishing, they caught 21 salmon trout and returned...*

Nathaniel Wyeth (16)

*Happening to have some knowledge of the habits of this fish I stepped down to the lower edge of the pond and placed myself on the shoal opposite to the deepest part in water a little over shoe mouth deep, and stood gun in hand, watching the appearance of the fish; presently, I saw it swimming down slowly close to the bottom, evidently uneasy at the presence of so many persons. As soon as it reached a depth of one foot, I aimed at his head and fired; a great splash of water followed, enveloping me and my gun. Before I could clear the water out of my eyes my comrades had the fish out on dry land, with a bullet hole through his head; he was a noble fish of the very largest size and in the finest condition.*

Warren Ferris (17)

Ferris learned a lesson from this incident. The next day, he tried to repeat this feat but could not do it, and was outfished by ten year old Indian boys who used sticks and stones. In fact, he said, the boys killed about three to every one of his, and he was using a double barreled gun which helped cut down reloading time.

He also wrote of some Indians who used lances to stick or pin the fish to the bottom of the stream. When they caught one, they would employ specially chosen sticks as stringers. The fish they caught were carried to the shore on forked sticks by hooking through the gills. Ferris and his men caught so many over the next few days that they thought their camps smelled like fish for months afterward. (18)

*...we arose in the morning and found ourselves in the valley of the east fork [Lemhi] of the Salmon River...we like wise saw numbers of salmon, forcing their way up the small streams, in this valley - many had so worn out their fins, that they could with difficulty avoid us when we endeavored to catch them, in our hands.*

Warren Ferris (19)

Small time fishing expeditions were nothing compared to the company Osborne Russell joined when heading west. He signed up with Nathaniel Wyeth and the *"Columbia River Fishing and Trading Company"* which planned to set up a salmon fishing business and ship the catch to the east coast in barrels of ice. Wyeth had planned for a large boat to be waiting for him when he arrived in Oregon to ship the catch east. But like many well thought out plans, a number of events conspired to make his plan fail, and the venture did not come to fruition.

While fishing was done all year long, you will note that some of these entries were done in the fall, when the annual upstream runs occurred. Everyone gathered all the food they could to prepare for approaching winter and this fine, tasty meat was a part of that.

The western Indian tribes had been catching fish long before any whites showed up and before they had any modern hooks. Zenas Leonard wrote Captain Walker and his men found a tribe of Indians who used the leg bone of a Sand Hill Crane, which is about eighteen inches long, fastening it to the end of a spearing pole. They would use these spears while floating on a raft made of rushes, and could kill fish at great distances with this tool. They also formed hooks from a crane's leg bone, which were ground down with sandstone. These had double barbs on it cut with a piece of flint and were used with flax lines. The line was tied to the nearest barbed end of the hook and by pulling the line, the sharp end of the hook caught in the fish's mouth when it turned sideways. (20)

Paul Kane (21) shows us a nice picture of Indians using torches while paddling quietly in a canoe to spear fish at night. The use of a torch gave them an opportunity to take the fish when they came to the surface. I do not know if it was the light, or the bugs that were drawn to the light which drew the fish, or if the light just helped them see the fish near the water's surface.

Kane also shows a picture of netting fish. (22) David Thompson in his *Columbia Journals* told of how they also used nets to catch fish. (23) Alexander Ross gave a great reference on how an assembly line was made to catch, cook and eat fish. Each man did a single job – one caught and flung it on the bank, one killed and cleaned it, one started and kept the small fire going and did the cooking. (24)

*Here [Twelve Mile Creek] we caught plenty of fish…*

Jacob Robinson (25)

Fishing in the west was not an everyday occurrence. The men usually had different animals on their mind when they viewed the water and what was in it, like beaver and its sign. But when the opportunity showed itself, no one was above taking a few fish. This kind of meat was good for them, tasted great and a healthy change from their daily diet. One other angle made this nice for the men – for most, it usually did not require any powder and ball to get it.

Fresh fish is an underutilized food source in many modern reenactment camps. But it should not be, for it is well documented and tastes fine by the campfire.

Fishing Accessory inventory listings:
- 500 fish hooks "Goods left of Fort Hall", 1834
- 3 bundles fishing line, Invoice of merchandise shipped on Steamboat Diana, 1835
- 1 paper fish hooks, James Baird estate
- doz hooks, sold to T Vergel & Isac Gilbredth, at 1825 rendezvous
- 3 doz fish hooks, to James Gardner, 1825 rendezvous
- 1/2 doz hooks, to Mr. Prudum, 1825 rendezvous
- doz hooks, Mr. Lolo, 1825 rendezvous
- 1/2 doz hooks, Mr. Montour

1. Terry Russell, *Messages from the President on the State of the Fur trade*, 1824- 1832, Ye Galleon Press, 1985, page 74.
2. Nathaniel Wyeth, *The Journals of Captain Nathaniel J. Wyeth's Expeditions to the Oregon Country, 1831-1836*, Ye Galleon Press, Fairfield, 1997, page 17.
3. Wyeth, page 21.
4. Wyeth, pages 22-3.
5. John Kirk Townsend, *Across the Rockies to the Columbia*, University of Nebraska Press, Lincoln, 1978, pages 84-5.
6. Townsend, page 99.
7. Zenas Leonard, *Adventures of a Mountain Man*, Milo Quaife editor, University of Nebraska Press, Lincoln, 1978, page 6.
8. Jedediah Smith, *A Southwest Expedition of Jedediah Smith*, University of Nebraska Press, Lincoln, 1989, pages 70-1.
9. Townsend, page 255.
10. Narcissa Whitman, *My Journal*, University of Nebraska Press, Lincoln, 1989, *page 33*.
11. Osborne Russell, *Journal of a Trapper*, University of Nebraska Press, Lincoln, 1986 page 97.
12. Rufus Sage, *Rocky Mountain Life*, University of Nebraska Press, Lincoln, 1982, page 262.
13. Charles Murray, *Travels in North America*, William Blackwood and Sons, Edinburgh, 1900, page 143.
14. George Brewerton, *Overland with Kit Carson*, University of Nebraska Press, Lincoln, pages 110-1.
15. James Clyman, *Journal of a Mountain Man*, Mountain Press Publishing, Missoula,

1984, page 90.

16. Wyeth, page 17.

17. Warren Ferris, *Life in the Rocky Mountains,* Old West Publishing, Denver, 1983, pages 418-9.

18. Ferris, pages 418-9.

19. Ferris, page 228.

20. Leonard, pages 117-8.

21. Paul Kane, *Wanderings of an Artist,* Charles Tuttle Company, Rutland, 1968, pages 21-2.

22. Kane, page 70.

23. David Thompson, *Columbia Journals,* Barbara Belyea editor, University of Washington Press, Seattle, 1994, pages 110-1.

24. Alexander Ross, *Adventures of the First Settlers on the Oregon or Colombia River, 1810-1813,* University of Nebraska Press, Lincoln, 1986, pages 142-3.

25. Jacob Robinson, *The Journal of the Santa Fe Expedition,* Narrative Press, Santa Barbara, 2001, page 2.

# *Breads*

*It is said that one does not eat bread without butter. If you have a cake of wheat mixed with marrow, the best fat in the world, then you have something with which to regale your friends.*

Nicholas Point (1)

**B**READ has always been considered a rare treat in the west, but is actually mentioned much more in the primary sources than is assumed. Once a person was on the plains or even in the mountains, its ingredients were not easily kept usable while on the trail, or easily replaceable.

The main ingredient, flour, was hard to keep in good condition because of moisture's effects. River crossings, morning dews, afternoon rains and every other way of moisture you can think of left flour caked and unusable. Plus, getting the leavened bread to rise was exceptionally hard to do in the outdoors, no matter how low the humidity was – unless you had an oven of some kind. This made non-rising crackers, small biscuits and forms of trail bread much sought after and relished.

Bread does not have a quick cooking time like meat and takes a while to make properly, which is why simpler breads like tortillas, dumplings and pancakes can be found in the journals. They were much easier to make – non-rising lumps for the most part, and they were made of usually only flour and water.

You will recognize by the end of this chapter that there are a number of entries that tell us about bread or a bread substitute. The following entries are only from a few good historical books found in my library. Bread-type foods were in more common use than I had previously thought. Having said this, I need to point out that the percentage of days when this staple was eaten was very low.

*Over the culinary department presided of late years a fair lady of colour, Charlotte by name, who was as she loved to say "de onlee lady in de dam Injun country." And who moreover was celebrated from Long's Peak to the Cumbres Espanalas for slap-jacks and pumpkin pies.*

George Ruxton (2)

George Sibley, as we have seen in a previous chapter, brought 300 pounds of corn meal for him and his men while surveying the Santa Fe Trail. (3) This was used not only for breads, but to coat meat for frying.

Cost was a factor with flour's use for the men who came across its availability at the forts and rendezvous:

*Best of all, I had means to accomplish my journey; for, out of my wages of $296 I had saved over $200, thanks to not indulging too much in pancake parties. Coffee being $1 a pint, sugar $1, and flour 25 cents, many of my poor comrades came out in debt.*

Charles Larpenteur (4)

*We reached Fort Bois…There are some flour and Indian meal to be sold here; seven pounds of flour for a dollar – mountain price!*

Joseph Williams (5)

These entries were written about flour that came from the east. There were other options. It seems there were two kinds of flour available in the west; a "superfine" and a coarser Spanish flour, found at a few forts and in the southwestern settlements. The white finely ground was sold for $40.00 a barrel and ten dollars less for the Spanish.

*We bought here some Spanish Flour, which rather deserved to be called bran; but as our appetite was none too squeamish, we enjoyed it immensely.*

Fredrick Wislizenus (6)

*Our people were supplied with food and shelter from the rain which is constant they raise at this fort 6000 bush. of wheat 3,000 of Barley...*

Nathaniel Wyeth (7)

*The next day I hired a Mexican to carry some flour back to meet the wagons; for our party was by this time running short of provisions.*

Josiah Gregg (8)

A wide, and surprising, variety of native plants were used by various groups to make types of bread. Here are just a few examples:

*The Honey Locust of this country bears a pod somewhat longer than a bean. The Indians gather these and pound both the pod and the bean it contains until it forms a coarse flour. They work it into loaves and let it dry, it is then fit for use. When they use it, they rinse it with water to which it imparts a sweet and yet tartish taste by no means unpleasant...their method of grinding their wheat is somewhat tedious. On a larger flat stone a little concave it is pounded or rather rolled with another stone in the shape of a bakers rolling pin until it is sufficiently fine...the bread which they form of this meal is baked in the sand or ashes under the fire without the covering of bark or grass used by the Pawnees.*

Jedediah Smith (9)

*...fried bread, which was a luxury. Mountain bread is simply coarse flour & water mixed, & roasted or fried in buffalo grease. To one who has nothing but meat for a long time this relishes very well!*

Narcissa Whitman (10)

The camas root, discussed in the following chapter on vegetables, was also used as a bread substitute.

A version of bread that was very popular at this time was called by various names (cracker, "pancake" or a "cake"). It was very easy to make, no rising of the bread, quick to make and eat and did not require any finesse to make edible. The most unsought after version of this was the army kind:

*After the boat landed, three barrels of hard-tack were put ashore, with some sugar and coffee and given to the Indian soldiers...*

Charles Larpenteur (11)

E. Willard Smith noted that his *"pancakes"* were only flour and water mixed and baked in a pan. (12) Charles Murray wrote his flour cakes were fried in bacon grease. (13) This combination (flour and water) was the most common form noted, not in a disagreeable manner, but as being different than what they had eaten in more "civilized" places.

*Had a present to-night of a fresh salmon; also a plate of fried cakes from Mr. McLeod. (Girls, if you wish to know how they taste you can have pleasure by taking a little flour and water, make some dough, and roll it thin, cut it into square blocks, then take some beef fat and fry them. You need not put either salt or pearlash in your dough.)*

Narcissa Whitman (14)

*As much could not be said in favor of the bread. It was little more than a paste made of flour and water, and fried like fritters, in lard; though some adapted a ruder style, twisting it round the ends of sticks, and thus roasting it before the fire. In either way, I found it extremely palatable on the prairies. No one knows the true relish of food until he has a hunter's appetite.*

Washington Irving (15)

*The day we moved in was a holiday, and in the evening a great feast was given us by Mr. Campbell – Mr. Sublette having left in the keel boat a few days after our arrival, taking ten men with him. It consisted of half a pint of flour to each men, one cup of coffee, one of sugar, and one of molasses to four men. Out of this a becoming feast was made, consisting of thick pancakes, the batter containing not another ingredient than pure Missouri water, greased with buffalo tallow; but as I had had nothing of the kind for upward of six months, I thought I had never tasted anything so good in my life and swore I would have plenty of the like if I ever got back to the states.*

Charles Larpenteur (16)

*We have purchased about 4 bushells of rice and flour in camp for cases of extremity...*

Nathaniel Wyeth (17)

We can see it was a major outlay for a person to make anything like bread, so when a greenhorn at a rendezvous says, *"He promised to make some dumplings and I have bought sugar and flour and some brandy!"* his friends made him keep his promise. (18)

*...in consisting of tea Cakes butter milk dried meat etc I eat very sparingly*

*as I had been three days fasting but drank so much strong tea that it kept me awake till after midnight...*

Osborne Russell (19)

*When the supplies were brought up in the Summer, about two pounds of bread each, for one-hundred men were brought in for the feast, made once a year, - and only then did they have bread.*

Robert Campbell (20)

*"...we found our biscuit and crackers almost all ruined."*

Zebulon Pike (21)

*In front of many dwellings is a mud oven, in the shape like a cupping glass, in which is baked the whitest bread it has ever been my fortune to taste. No bolting cloths are here used and those wanting white bread sift for themselves. The hard bread, biscoche, is light, and sweet- a luxury with a cup of coffee by a mountain pine fire.*

Lewis Garrard (22)

*They gave us food as they had consisting of a kind of mush made of acorns and pine nuts bread made of a small berry. This bread in appearance was like corn bread but in taste much sweeter.*

Jedediah Smith (23)

*A specimen of the bread root (psoralea esculenta), was procured from the creek-bank by one of the voyagers. This is very common in the vicinity of the mountains, and attains a size from twenty to thirty inches in circumference. It is taprooted and generally prefers the rich sandy soil of bottoms and ravines...in shape, it is much like the common beet. It exterior is covered with a thick ligament of tough fibrous, curiously interwoven, enveloping a white pulpy substance, which is very sweet and pleasantly tasted.*

Rufus Sage (24)

*...they returned bringing some loaves of bread weighing each 8 or 10 pounds. It was so hard that an ax was required to break it and in taste resembled Sugar Candy. .. I found it was made of cane grass...*

Jedediah Smith (25)

All the breads found on these pages should not be overlooked in the recreated modern camp setting. They should be used in small amounts and with reference to where you are and what you are recreating. Other than that,

**45**

they fill a void that other food staples cannot.

> *...for weeks past, a traveling Babel, leaped for joy as the gates of the fort were thrown open; and "welcome to Fort William" – the hearty welcome of fellow countrymen in the wild wilderness- greeted us. Peace again – roofs again- safety again from the winged arrows of the savage- relief again from the depraved suggestions of in humanity – bread, ah! Bread again...*

Thomas Farnham (26)

> *...here let me say there was one young lady which showed herself worthy of the bravest undaunted pioneer of the west for after having kneaded her dough she watched and nursed the fire and held an umbrella over the fire and her skillet with the greatest composure for near 2 hours and baked bread enough to us a very plentiful supper...*

James Clyman (27)

> *Our food consisted of bacon, and bread, made of flour and water formed into a paste and baked in a frying pan.*

E. Willard Smith (28)

> *This night our rations were reduced to one-eighth of a pint of flour to each man. This, as our custom was, was kneaded with water, and baked or rather fried in our frying pan over a fire sufficiently destitute of combustibles to have satisfied the most fastidious miser in that line.*

Thomas Farnham (29)

I will underscore this thought that bread was a great addition to any meal and not just *"a filler"* as it was written about. (30) Joseph Williams thought the meat-only diet with no bread had weakened his body. Everybody may not have liked the quality of the bread they were served, but they did not turn it down.

1. Nicholas Point, *Wilderness Kingdom*, Loyola Press, Chicago, 1967, page 129.
2. George Ruxton, *Life in the Far West*, LeRoy Hafen editor, University of Oklahoma Press, Norman, 1985, page 180.
3. George Sibley, *The Road to Santa Fe*, Kate Gregg editor, University of New Mexico Press, Albuquerque, 1968, page 176
4. Charles Larpenteur, *Forty Years a Fur Trader on the Upper Missouri*, University of Nebraska Press, Lincoln, 1989, page 51.
5. Joseph Williams, *Narrative of a Tour from the State of Indiana to the Oregon Territory*

*in the Years 1841-2*, Ye Galleon Press, Fairfield, 1977, page 33.

6. Dr. Fredrick Wislizenus, *A Journey to the Rocky Mountains in the Year 1839*, Ye Galleon Press, Fairfield, 1989, page 141.

7. Nathaniel J. Wyeth, *The Journals of Captain Nathaniel J. Wyeth's Expeditions to the Oregon Country, 1831-1836*, Ye Galleon Press, Fairfield, 1997, page 30.

8. Josiah Gregg, *Commerce of the Prairies*, University of Nebraska Press, Lincoln, 1967, page 226.

9. Jedediah Smith's Journal - *First Expedition to California, a Southwest Expedition of Jedediah Smith*, University of Nebraska Press, Lincoln, 1989, pages 75-6.

10. Narcissa Whitman, *My Journal*, University of Nebraska Press, Lincoln, 1989, pages 20-1.

11. Larpenteur, page 243.

12. E. Willard Smith, Colorado Magazine, *With the Fur Traders of Colorado*, July 1950, page 164.

13. Charles Murray, *Travels in North America*, William Blackwood and Sons, Edinburgh, 1900, page 290.

14. Whitman, page 27.

15. Washington Irving, *A Tour of the Prairies*, University of Oklahoma Press, Norman, 1971, pages 57-8.

16. Larpenteur, pages 42-3.

17. Wyeth, page 88.

18. Sir William Drummond Stewart, *Edward Warren*, Mountain Press, Missoula, 1986, page 216.

19. Osborne Russell, *Journal of a Trapper*, University of Nebraska Press, Lincoln, 1986, page 108.

20. Robert Campbell, *A Narrative of Colonel Robert Campbell's, Experiences in the Rocky Mountain Fur Trade from 1825-1835*, Drew Hollway, editor, Ye Galleon Press, Fairfield, Washington, 1999, page 23.

21. Zebulon Pike, *The Southwest Journals of Zebulon Pike*, Stephen Hart & Archer Hulbert editors, University of New Mexico Press, Albuquerque, 2006, page 88.

22. Lewis Garrard, *Wah-to-yah and the Taos Trail*, University of Oklahoma Press, Norman, 1957, page 175.

23. Smith, page 92.

24. Rufus Sage, *Rocky Mountain Life*, University of Nebraska Press, Lincoln, 1982, page 76.

25. Smith, page 90. [Note on this said it was baked screw mesquite loaves.]

26. Thomas Farnham, *Travels in the Great Western Prairies, the Anahuac and Rocky Mountains, and in the Oregon Territory*, private printing, Bob Elsloo and Don Erickson, 2009, page 40.

27. James Clyman, *Journal of a Mountain Man*, Mountain Press Publishing, Missoula, 1984, page 75.

28. Smith, page 164.
29. Farnham, page 21.
30. Joseph Williams, *Narrative of a Tour from the State of Indiana to the Oregon Territory in the Years 1841-2*, Ye Galleon Press, Fairfield, 1977, page 33.

A Native Garden.

# Vegetables

*Stopped 2 hours took breakfast they [the Mandan] presented me
some dry corn and some roasting ears. All these villages cultivate corn peas
beans pumpkins etc...*

Nathaniel Wyeth (1)

**T**HE people of the 1800's did not refer to the triangle food chart
put out by the USDA when planning their meals. What was
available was what was eaten. Vegetables were found in their
diet, but not in the quantities or frequency that we have. No one
that I know of was a vegetarian in the west – well, maybe one out of 5-6,000
individuals I know of – Audubon. (2)

But that last statement doesn't say all that I want to on this topic. All of the forts tried to raise crops to supplement their diets; some were more successful than others in this. The soil and length of growing seasons limited what they could do in this area. And the ones located in the more northern, central climates had a much harder time with growing vegetables. Joseph Williams commented that even the missionary stations had gardens with all kinds of vegetables in it. (3)

Alexander Barclay did list in his journal what he planted in his gardens while he lived at his small enclosed hacienda he called "Hardscrabble":

*April 29th, began ploughing [plowing]*

*30th, ploughing- planted yellow corn, the earliest- & some melon & pumpkin seed.*

*May 4th ploughing- planted radishes & black-eyed peas & onions-*

*12th, Planted melon, radish and &...*

*17th, planted some radishes, black-eyed peas, peaches, plums. Cherries and &... (4)*

Fresh vegetables were also to be had at Ft. Pierre, and found in a number of places in the west:

*I remained all this day eating and drinking of the good things afforded by the earth and the cellars of the Co. Found cucumbers water & musk mellons beets carrots potatoes onions corn and a good cabin and the Company of Mr. Laidlow and Doct.*

Nathaniel Wyeth (5)

*But men accustomed to living on meat and at the same time traveling hard will eat a surprising quantity of corn and beans, which at this time constituted our principle substance.*

Jedediah Smith (6)

Many Native Tribes did the same. Beans, corn and melons were described as being grown by the Paiutes in Smith's journal:

*...producing melons and corn...Their wheat is planted in hills...at this season are fed on pumpkins and melons of which they appear very fond...melons were supplied in such numbers that I had frequently 3 or 400 piled up before my tent.*

Jedediah Smith (7)

*They made a kind of earthen ware and in large crock of this they boil their beans, corn, pumpkin & c.*

Jedediah Smith (8)

*When the steamboat stopped to take in fuel, I went ashore and gathered some fine ripe pawpaw; this was the first time that I had tasted this fruit, which in, in my opinion, one the most delicious in the world. It resembles very much the banana of the West Indies, but is more rich and luscious. There are two species, the green and the yellow the latter is preferable. When opened, the interior is exactly like a custard, and the flavor is something between a fig and an pine apple…I find it is not generally so highly esteemed, being considered too rich and cloying; moreover I was told it is extremely unwholesome. This I found to be an absurd prejudice, as I have often eaten from six to twelve at a time without any unpleasant consequence.*

Charles Murray (9)

*We observed very many bitter herbs, especially wormwood; also Pomme Blanche (psoralea esculenta), whose knobby roots contains much starch, has a pleasant taste, and is gathered by the Indians.*

Fredrick Wislizenus (10)

The Mandan grew corn, peas, beans, pumpkins. Wyeth's journal tells us that the Mandan presented him some dried corn and some roasting ears. They had already had some of this "green" [not dried] corn and were roasting it. (11)

*Mr. N. and myself walked over the farm with the doctor, to inspect the various improvements which he has made. He has already several hundred acres fenced in and under cultivation, and like our own western prairieland, it produces abundant crops, particularly of grain, without requiring any manure. Wheat thrives astonishingly; I never saw better in any country and the various culinary vegetables, potatoes, carrots, parsnips and & c. are in great profusion, and of the first quality.*

John Townsend (12)

*[Doctor McLaughan (sp)] is doing much good here by introducing fruits into this country which will much facilitate the progress of the settlement (Indian corn 300 bushels)…*

Nathaniel Wyeth (13)

*They [the people at Pecos] raise onions, peas, beans, corn, wheat and red pepper – the last a principal ingredient in Spanish food. .. their gardens are enclosed.*

Thomas James (14)

*…the inhabitants of the village cultivate about one hundred and fifty acres of land in corn, beans, pumpkins, melons…*

Anthony Glass (15)

*51*

A different form of food in this class of natural growing vegetables was the Camas root. It is one of those foods which are hard to categorize. What the native growing plant was and how it was used is described in the following passages:

*Of these, the principal was an esculent root, something between a potato and a radish, most greedily sought by the Indians when going into buffalo country: they are then often reduced to a state approaching to starvation; and I have seen these roots dug out two, three and even four miles from the regular trail. I ate them, and they appear somewhat nutritious and not unpalatable, but under any other circumstances, would be thought tasteless and difficult of digestion. They are eaten raw, and I have never seen any attempt to cook them among the Pawnees: but they are said to be tolerably wholesome as well as palatable when boiled or roasted. The Canadian French call them Pomme blanche; their Pawnee name I forget, but in the Ojibway dialect they are called Metus-ko-she-min or grass berries and their botanical appellation, I believe Psoralea eulenta.*

Sir Charles Murray (16)

[There is more I want to say about this plant and it will show up again in a later chapter.]

The early southern Indian trader, Anthony Glass, notes that the tribes he came in contact with always raised more than they could eat and traded the surplus for mules and horses. They transported the overage by cutting them up and when wilted, the pieces are tied with strings and woven into kind of a cloth. (17)

Joseph Nicollet came upon the ruins of building at Council Bluff and notes the garden was still coming up after the inhabitants had left:

*A vegetable garden planted on the sunny southern slope of the hill is remarkable for beautiful tufts of asparagus now grown to immense size. We enjoyed eating it we were delayed on the island of willows. There was some horse-radish, that condiment indispensible to the table of the American settler.* (18)

...and as our supply of beans was very low, our diet consisted almost exclusively of maize boiled in water, which greatly weakened our digestion.

Prince Maximilian (19)

*...we found a little arbour already made...and the pilaffe (pilaf or rice) with a few slices of ham and a bull's tongue, set off what was intended to be the*

*last of our scanty meals.*

Sir William Drummond Stewart (20)

...there is plenty of wild parsnips here...

Nathaniel Wyeth (21)

*After trading with these Indians {the Pawnee] for some corn, we left them...*

Zenas Leonard (22)

*We saw some small spots cultivated, where corn, pumpkins, and beans are grown.*

John Audubon (23)

*The fort* [Vancouver] *has laid out a farm in the vicinity. In 1837, about three thousand acres were in cultivation. The produce was: 8,000 bushels of wheat, 5,500 bushels of barley, 6,000 bushels of oats, 9,000 bushels of peas and 4,000 bushels of potatoes.*

Fredrick Wislizenus (24)

Vegetables are not something we associate with the early west, but they were found and eaten there. The entries listed give more than enough proof that they were commonplace in the west; especially by the native tribes who were not as nomadic as others. We do see that whites, as they settled in permanent locations, always tried to duplicate what was grown in the land where they came from and the foods found there, so they grew as similar as possible vegetables to complement their stores. Even Marcy, in his words of how to prepare for the trip, thought wild onions an excellent anti-scorbutic and an antidote for scurvy. (25) So, they not only added to the everyday diet of the route, vegetables could also help increase the percentage of those healthy enough to complete the journey.

1.  Nathaniel J. Wyeth, *The Journals of Captain Nathaniel J. Wyeth's Expeditions to the Oregon Country, 1831-1836,* Ye Galleon Press, Fairfield, 1997, page 65.
2.  Maria R. Audubon, *Audubon and His Journals,* Elloitt Coues editor, Dover Publications, New York, 1994, pages 22-3.
3.  Joseph Williams, *Narrative of a Tour from the State of Indiana to the Oregon Territory in the Years 1841-2,* Ye Galleon Press, Fairfield, 1977, page 34.
4.  Alexander Barclay, *Mountain Man,* George Hammond, Old West Publishing, Denver, Colorado, 1976, page 138.
5.  Wyeth, page 67.

6.   Jedediah Smith, *a Southwest Expedition of Jedediah Smith*, University of Nebraska Press, Lincoln, 1989, page 90.
7.   Smith, page 83.
8.   Smith, page 75.
9.   Charles Murray, *Travels in North America*, William Blackwood and Sons, Edinburgh, 1900, page 348.
10.  Dr. Fredrick Wislizenus, *A Journey to the Rocky Mountains in the Year 1839*, Ye Galleon Press, Fairfield, 1989, page 61.
11.  Wyeth, page 65.
12.  John Townsend, *Across the Rockies to the Columbia*, University of Nebraska Press, Lincoln, 1978, page 188.
13.  Wyeth, page 31.
14.  Thomas James, *Three Years Among the Indians and Mexicans*, Milo Quaife editor, Citadel Press, New York, 1966, page 147.
15.  Dan Flores, *Journal of an Indian Trader*, Texas A & M, College Station, 1985, page 48.
16.  Murray, page 152-3.
17.  Flores, page 55.
18.  Joseph Nicollet, *Joseph N. Nicollet on the Plains and Prairies,* Edmund and Martha Bray editors, Minnesota Historical Society, St. Paul, 1993, page 149.
19.  Prince Maximilian, *People of the First Man*, Davis Thomas & Karin Ronnefeldt editors, Promontory Press, 1982, pages 201.
20.  Sir William Drummond Stewart, *Edward Warren*, Mountain Press, Missoula, 1986, pages 81, 87 (n).
21.  Wyeth, page 93.
22.  Zenas Leonard, *Adventures of a Mountain Man*, Milo Quaife editor, University of Nebraska Press, Lincoln, 1978, page 263.
23.  Audubon, page 10.
24.  Wislizenus, page 111.
25.  Randolph Marcy, *The Prairie Traveler*, Applewood Books, Bedford, 1993, page 33.

A tea pot on the hearth.

# *Teas*

*…as I had been three days fasting but drank so much strong tea that it kept me awake till after midnight…*

Osborne Russell (1)

**D**URING the Fur Trade years, tea was a popular drink. Invigorating, sometimes with a high caffeine content, one pound of tea leaves makes more servings than a pound of any other substance known to man.

Much of the tea was from China. This tea was basically divided into two groups: green tea and black tea. Charles Larpenteur was one of the more well known of the many tea drinkers. A small canister of tea was found in James Baird's estate inventory. (2) We see this drink found in merchandise lists of the Missouri Fur Company and others.

*After dressing ourselves and giving a brief history and sufferings; supper was brought in consisting of Tea, Cakes, butter, milk, dried meat...*

Osborne Russell (3)

Loose "Gunpowder" Tea.

Besides the more common teas, we find writings on some natural teas used when men ran out of the purchased ones in their supplies.

*In this vicinity a species of shrub, which I had before noticed in various places, (designated as "red-root" by our voyageurs,) became quite abundant. The red-root is highly esteemed as a substitute for tea, and my own experience attests its superiority of flavor to any article of that kind imported from China. In appearance it is very similar to the tea of commerce, and it affords at all times a most excellent beverage. It is found only upon the prairies between the frontiers and Big Blue, and in some portions of the Rocky Mountains.*

Rufus Sage (4)

*For tea we had the same, with the addition of some stewed service berries.*

Narcissa Whitman (5)

*...a fire was struck, and kettle of tea prepared from wild cherry bark, which proved quite wholesome.*

Rufus Sage (6)

*They [our cattle] are a source of great comfort to us in this land of scarcity. They supply us with sufficient milk for our tea & coffee which is indeed a luxury.*

Narcissa Whitman (7)

Teas are light to carry, can be used to make more than one cup, and unlike coffee beans, do not require cooking before using. Again, it was definitely not the most-used drink in the west, but one which was common enough to be documented. It turns up in various inventory documents under various names. If you are like me and enjoy a cup of this steaming liquid, don't be afraid to use it in your camps.

*My stock of bread, sugar and tea, is completely spoiled by the salt water...*

John Townsend (8)

1.  Osborne Russell *Journal of a Trapper*, University of Nebraska Press, Lincoln, 1986, page 108.
2.  Mike Moore, *Heroes to Me*, Historical Enterprises, Macon Georgia, 2003, page 59.
3.  Osborne Russell, *Journal of a Trapper*, University of Nebraska Press, Lincoln, 1986, page 108.
4.  Rufus Sage, *Rocky Mountain Life*, University of Nebraska Press, Lincoln, 1982, page 147.
5.  Narcissa Whitman, My *Journal*, University of Nebraska Press, Lincoln, 1989, page 20.
6.  Sage, page 147.
7.  Whitman, page 17.
8.  John Townsend, *Across the Rockies to the Columbia*, University of Nebraska Press, Lincoln, 1978, page 257.

Green coffee beans roasting.

# Coffee

| | |
|---|---|
| *First cache:* | *2 bags coffee* |
| *Second cache:* | *3 Bags coffee* |
| | *200 lbs.* |

William Ashley (1)

**I**N those days, one thing was different than today for the men when traveling: they usually only ate twice a day. A quick cup of coffee for breakfast, then a liquid and dried meat while in the saddle, a break at noon to rest the horses and men, with the main meal at evening.

With these times of refreshment, coffee seems to be the main item served with all meals, when it was available. They did not have the instant or canned, packaged or ground beans as see used today. Coffee beans that were sent west were green.

Another interesting thing is that coffee and sugar were used in equal quantities and show up together in the Ashley account books to many of the trappers at the first rendezvous. (2)

> *The hard bread, biscoche, is light, porous and sweet – a perfect luxury with a cup of coffee by a mountain fire. Probably long contained abstinence from all kinds of farinaceous food influenced my judgment – but without a doubt, it would meet with favor at the Planter's House…*
>
> Lewis Garrard (3)

Just like today, we see a few combinations with the dark liquid. Not "donuts and coffee," but "Mush and coffee." Garrard seems to have liked this and he again comments on sitting down, after the animals were safe and hobbled, to a snack of beef with biscoche soaked in "java" from the time-honored little tin kettle they used. (4) Earlier in his book he wrote that they untied their tin cups from the saddles, which they filled with ingredients from a coffeepot, and had dried buffalo meat, before turning in for the night. (5)

> *Indeed our coffee, which, as long as it held out, had been served up with every meal, according to the custom of the West, was by no means a beverage to boast of. It was roasted in a frying pan, without much care, pounded in a leathern bag, with a round stone, and boiled in our prime and almost only kitchen utensil, the camp-kettle, in "branch" or brook water: which, on the prairies, is deeply colored by the soil, of which it always holds abundant particles in a state of solution and suspension. In fact, in the course of our tour, we had tasted the quality of every variety of soil, and the draughts of water we had taken might vie in color, if not flavor, with the tinctures of an apothecary's shop. Pure, limpid water is a rare luxury on the prairies, at least at this season of the year.*
>
> Washington Irving (6)

Coffee was sometimes sweetened if possible, with sugar or molasses or honey, for some did not like it straight and strong. (7) Lewis Garrard also gave us the price he paid for the beans when he could find them (8) – the coffee they had cost them $1.00 a pound, the sugar they used in it cost the same. Lewis is not the only one to mention the high price of this. Charles Larpenteur laments:

> *…the cost of such luxuries like sugar, flour and coffee…* (9)

> *Here [Bent's Fort] I bought some sugar and coffee, for each of which I gave two dollars a pound!*
>
> Joseph Williams (10)

John Audubon, in his *Western Journals*, complains about the price, which was almost a half a day's pay: *We paid fifty cents for a cup of coffee and a bit of bread...* (11)

How did they actually make coffee on the trail?

*That night, the coffee gave out. We had nothing in which to burn more, but as necessity is ever the mother of invention, we selected two flat stones from the channel at hand, twenty five to thirty inches in diameter, which we placed on the fire till heated, then one was taken off, the coffee poured on, and stirred with a stick. The stones served alternately as they became cool. When the coffee was sufficiently burned, a piece of skin was laid on the ground and clean stone, a foot in diameter, rested on the knees of the grinder, with one edge on the skin. A smaller stone, held in the hand, reduced the grains between it and the larger one to powder by a rotary action.*

Lewis Garrard (12)

Some green coffee beans are shown cooking in the photograph at the beginning of this chapter. They are kind of a light green in color that changes in darkness while cooking. This color gives you a hint when they are ready to use. Some like to taste the bean, I usually go by color and how long I can stand to roast them, since it is not a quick process. You must stir them from time to time and flip them if possible get them completely cooked.

The coffee bean was actually not an item which the whites introduced into the west. Lt. James Abert wrote about a band of Indians they met, who Tom Fitzpatrick calls the "Buffalo Eaters":

*When coffee was given to them, one when who before raising his cup to his lips, dipped his finger in the cup and crossed himself, in imitation of what he had seen done by the Spaniards, with whom they hold some intercourse.* (13)

Afterwards Abert notes that he did not think these Indians appeared to relish the coffee.

*...After having starved 24 hours hear we wormed our selvs and dried our things and had to mack our colfy in 2 tin cups as we had the misforntun of mr seglar hors a foling on the ice as we was crossing the Fk of rawhid it smashed our cofipot sow we had to throw it away the 2 cups of cofy that I mad this morning I thot it was the best that I evr drunk.*

David Adams (14)

Another who commented on the quality of the coffee served was James Clyman:

*And here I again obtained a cup of excellent coffee at Judge Morin's camp the first I had tasted since the early part of the last winter.* [It was June 26th when he wrote this, what is the expression – absence makes the heart fonder?] (15)

Henry Brewer notes while on a stopover at Rio de Janeiro that the coffee trade between that country and the United States in 1843 was $10 million each year. (16) William Ashley's Notebook from the 1825 Rendezvous shows sugar and coffee being important sales items to trappers.

*To economize our stock of coffee, we were forced to make it wretchedly weak, and for the want of sugar or molasses to sweeten it with honey, of which we had about twenty pounds.*

Prince Maximilian (17)

*...with all this our beverage was coffee, boiled in a camp kettle, sweetened with brown sugar and drunk out of a tin cups...*

Washington Irving (18)

*...he was all a lone sow I made a cup of cofy and invied solomon to partake sum with us which he did    Cofy is a luckary in the country...*

David Adams (19)

Even Matthew Field has some good lines on a pot of hot coffee and choicest parts of a freshly killed cow cooked over buffalo chips, which he described as toasted with such exhilaration as you would have thought it was fine wine. (20)

Coffee was what many considered a staple and when not available:

*The absence of coffee he made the theme of regret at every meal, bewailing his misfortune in not having at that particular moment a supply of this article, which he never before was without, and which I may here observe, amongst the hunters and trappers when in camp or rendezvous, is considered as an indispensible necessary. Coffee, being very cheap in the states, is the universal beverage of the western people, and find its way to the packs of the Indian Traders, who retail it to the mountain man at the moderate price of from two to six dollars the half pint cup.*

George Ruxton (21)

This drink was popular, warm, smelled good when cooking,

so use it heartily!

1.  Dale Morgan, *The West of William H. Ashley*, Old West Publishing Company, Denver, Colorado, 1964, *pages 107 & 112.*
2.  Morgan, pages 118-9.
3.  Lewis Garrard, *Wah-to-yah and the Taos Trail*, University of Oklahoma Press, Norman, 1957, page 175.
4.  Garrard, page 203.
5.  Garrard, page 46.
6.  Irving, page 247.
7.  Garrard, page 49.
8.  Garrard, page 60.
9.  Charles Larpenteur, *Forty Years a Fur Trader on the Upper Missouri*, University of Nebraska Press, Lincoln, 1989, page 51.
10. Joseph Williams, *Narrative of a Tour from the State of Indiana to the Oregon Territory in the Years 1841-2*, Ye Galleon Press, Fairfield, 1977, page 56.
11. John Audubon, *Audubon's Western Journal*, University of Arizona Press, Tucson, 1984, page 190.
12. Washington Irving, *A Tour of the Prairies*, University of Oklahoma Press, Norman, 1971, page 196.
13. Lt. James Abert, *Expedition to the Southwest*, University of Nebraska Press, Lincoln, 1999, page 60.
14. *The David Adams Journals*, Charles Hanson, Jr. editor, Museum of the Fur Trade, Chadron, 1994, page 23.
15. James Clyman, *Journal of a Mountain Man*, Mountain Press Publishing, Missoula, 1984, page 261.
16. Henry Brewer, *The Journals of Henry Brewer*, Richard Seiber editor, Ye Galleon Press, Fairfield, 1986, page 35.
17. Prince Maximilian, *People of the First Man*, Davis Thomas & Karin Ronnefeldt editors, Promontory Press, New York, 1982, page 200.
18. Washington Irving, *Adventures of Captain Bonneville*, University of Oklahoma Press, Norman, 1971, pages 59-9.
19. Adams, page 76.
20. Matthew Field, *Matt Field on the Santa Fe Trail*, John Sunder editor, University of Oklahoma Press, Norman, 1995, page 142.
21. George Ruxton, *Ruxton of the Rockies*, LeRoy Hafen editor, University of Oklahoma Press, Norman, 1982, page 197.

# *Water*

*They* [the employees at Bent's Fort] *have a well inside, and fine water it is – especially with ice.*

Susan Magoffin (1)

**W**HEN coffee and tea ran out, the only option left to the individuals living in the west was plain old water. Liquor of all kinds may quench one form of thirst, coffee and tea were looked forward to; but for the most important desire man has only water would do.

Water was the largest percentage of all liquids consumed by every ethnic group and their animals during this time frame. Water, unlike today, has many different looks and tastes. In our modern world, we sanitize it, add chemicals to it and filter it. Not so with water 175 years ago. Every creek, river, spring and stream not only looked different, but tasted different. The soil around it and sometimes in it, added to the varying smell, looks and taste.

Dr. Fredrick Wislizenus comments on a spring he had just tasted:

# Foods of the Early American West

*We left the Beer Spring on the morning of August 14th. I drank some cups of the sparkling water, and bade adieu to the place so endeared to me as to an old friend that one does not expect to see again for a long time.* (2)

Many times, the travelers moved away from flowing sources and had to rely on other methods to keep themselves and their animals hydrated. Water was hunted for, gathered, kept like any other ingredient, and carried with them, too.

*We ate our scanty suppers, drank water from the puddles and sought rest.*
Thomas Farnham (3)

Methods which helped them transport water include powder horns, small kegs and barrels. But other ways are also seen – Jedediah Smith noted he had seen Indians carry water in an antelope bladder.

*After crossing the Salt Plain I found a place where there was water and some grass and encamped. The water was in holes dug about two feet deep and quite brackish making some new holes I found the water some better.*
Jedediah Smith (4)

*...and desiring the men to fill two empty bottles which remained to us with water, and to put some also into the coffee pot, we started in the direction of the buffalo track...*

Charles Murray (5)

All forts or trading houses had some source of water near or in them. Once wagons became the primary way of carrying heavy loads, they could carry larger containers of water in them. When you note a wagon in use, they usually had a barrel tied to the side of them. You will also note that the itineraries found in the guide books and the journals give the distances between campsites and river crossings; we see how much they relied on a water source and realize that finding drinkable water was a very important aspect of daily life in the American west.

*At the foot of a slope were several springs, and toward sunset I used to walk out that way, and seated on a bank or adobe ruin, watch the women procuring water...and with well-filled antique fashioned earthen jars- manufactured by Indians inhabiting the country...*

Lewis Garrard (6)

*Just before night, at the foot of a small hill, we found a little spring or rather a hole of water furnishing a very inadequate supply for after taking out some to cook with, I led the horses to it and they drank it all.*

Jedediah Smith (7)

*...but among my list of sundries I must not forget my water flask, which was a curiosity in its way, and as I have not taken out a patent for the invention, it may give some ingenious Yankee a new idea. It was a bottle made of porous leather which held half a gallon, and suffered just so much of the liquid to soak through as was requisite to keep the outside constantly wet, so that whenever I desired cool water I had only to hang up my flask, or expose it to a free current of air.*

George Brewerton (8)

Water is often overlooked by historians because it was so every day and natural to those who inhabited the timeframe. But where would the west be without H2O?

1.  Susan Magoffin, *Down the Santa Fe Trail and into Mexico*, Stella Drumm, editor, Yale University Press, New Haven, 1962, pages 60-1.
2.  Dr. Fredrick Wislizenus, *A Journey to the Rocky Mountains in the Year 1839*, Ye

Galleon Press, Fairfield, 1989, page 124.

3. Thomas Farnham, *Travels in the Great Western Prairies*, Private printing, Don Erickson, 2007, *page 20*.

4. Jedediah Smith, *A Southwest Expedition of Jedediah Smith*, University of Nebraska Press, Lincoln, 1989, page 88.

5. Charles Murray, *Travels in North America*, William Blackwood and Sons, Edinburgh, 1900, page 305.

6. Lewis Garrard, Wah-to-yah and the Taos Trail, University of Oklahoma Press, Norman, 1957, page 180.

7. Smith, page 87.

8. George Brewerton, *Overland with Kit Carson*, University of Nebraska, Lincoln, 1993, page 50.

Site of Simeon Turley's distillery.

# Alcoholic Beverages

*The morning after my arrival on the Arkansas, two men, named Harwood and Markhead - the latter one of the most daring and successful trappers that ever followed this adventurous mountain life, and whom I had intended to have hired as a guide to the valley of the Columbia the ensuing spring - started off to the settlement of New Mexico, with some packs of peltries, intending to bring back Taos whisky (a very profitable article of trade amongst the mountain-men) and some bags of flour and Indian meal.*

George Frederick Ruxton (1)

**H**ISTORICAL alcohol, its manufacture and consumption is often portrayed today in a black-and-white manner. It is either the ruin of many people or the blessing of the earth. In reality it was both, and is another of those complex historical subjects that should be studied, thought out carefully, and then discussed.

Whiskey was probably the favorite drink of many of the individuals in the west and we read of many forms of it in the journals and diaries. The liquor along the northern Rocky Mountain region came mostly up the Missouri on boats. Some non-native liquors were produced at Fort Union and it almost cost them their trading license. In the central and southern intermountain region, whiskey came from Taos and surrounding areas where it was made by a few displaced Kentuckians.

Simeon Turley and Isaac Graham were familiar with its manufacture and shipped sections of stills west for its production along with their regular orders of goods. This "fire water" as it was called because of it high alcoholic content which could produce huge flames when spit into a fire, started from wheat. Simeon had a unique triangle set of crops on his farm and each benefited from the others in the cycle. He raised wheat to made liquor, the wheat refuse went to his pigs, which he ate and also sold.

The stills that were at the southern edge of Taos and Arroyo Hondo weren't the only ones in the west. "Poteen" or a "Pass whiskey" was a brandy made in El Paso and shipped north. (2)

*In the evening we moistened our pipes with* hot stopping *or brandy & water, usually without sugar.*

William Fairholme (3)

Beside the annual rendezvous, another area in which liquor had a major part was at the noisy, crowded monte halls and taverns in the Santa Fe/Taos area. The proprietors found that selling drinks along with a game of cards helped their bottom line.

Liquor, trade whiskey and all forms of alcohol, were a special and sometimes not so pleasant piece of the western American puzzle. We know of many times when, just like today; individuals sat around a fire, drank socially and just told stories. The use of alcohol during times like this and place was all positive and fun.

This libation was also used to keep workers in debt (and connected with a certain company until the debt was paid), used to extend and increase trade activity and bring tribes into trade agreements.

As a social drinker myself, I find it hard to write about the negative aspects of this and not give a balanced view to it. Liquor in the west had both positive and negative effects. Many journal writers decried the use of it among the Indians and what it did to whites who had partaken too much in it. So much has been written by those that I cannot do as many historians do and gloss over it or not write about it. David Brown will be the first to give us his thoughts on this:

*"The first few days after our arrival at the rendezvous, were one continued scene of wild revelry and excitement. A quantity of liquor which we had brought along with us in order to give the hunters what is termed a* good spree, *was the immediate cause of this state of things.*

*It has always been the custom of the American Fur Company, to supply the persons in its employment, once a year, with a large amount of this pernicious stimulant; induced thereto, no doubt, by a knowledge that in the thoughtless and extravagant exhilaration, many of their best and most industrious trappers are led to squander away in a few short days the hard earned wages of whole years of almost incessant labor, danger and privation. It is really pitiable to see some of these poor fellows on recovering from a paraxism of frantic and self induced madness, in which they had spent everything coming to them on the books of the company, - to the amount very often of several hundred dollars, - and on the possession of which they had built their calculations of retiring from this wild and hazardous life, to the peaceful occupations of civilized society. In thus encouraging and furnishing the means of intoxication, it is not going too far to say, that many of these men have felt themselves defrauded and cheated out of their money by the company, whose interest it was to keep them in the country, and which is especially anxious to retain in its service, all such as are due a large sum, as the risk of life is very important...In case of death the Company becomes executor to the deceased, and in general they appear to have been poorly regarded for their trouble and exertions. I do not know how it is, but every man who has died in that country for the last twenty years, died in its debt, and many persons who the day and hour preceding their death, were thought to have a large sum due them on the books of the Company, have yet been found, incredible as it may appear, to have not only worth* nothing, *but a few dollars less that even that.*

David Brown (4)

*When paying for the roves, the traders, in measuring out the liquor in a tin half pint cup, thrust their thumbs or four fingers of the hand into the measure, in order that it may contain the less, or not infrequently fill the bottom with melted buffalo fat, with the same object. So greedy are the Indians, that they never discover the cheat, and once under the influence of the liquor, cannot distinguish between the first comparatively strong spirit and the following ones diluted five hundred percent, and poisonously drugged to boot.*

George Ruxton (5)

These quotes say a lot about the liquor trade in the early west. It was a major source of income for some and the dirge of others. The hidden side of this is that not much of the balance of views on this subject gets printed in the pages of history.

Rufus Sage wrote about six ways the buyers were cheated by

those selling it: the full strength brew was diluted with three parts water, selling the cup half full when the operator sees the purchaser will not know the difference because of his impaired state, holding the cup with two fingers in it when filling it up, having two different cups (one larger than the other) and switching the two when the time is right, and having some cups half full of tallow.

Rufus Sage goes on for a few pages (6) on the negative aspect of it in the west, particularity when it involved the Native tribes. In fact Rufus plainly states:

*The forgoing results of this infamous traffic, are only a few of the many instances of like nature I might cite, in proof of its imminent danger to those engaged in its prosecution- but this is not the darkest part of the picture. There are yet scenes in reserve, more bloody and dreadful than those recited...*

These were not missionaries or soft men from the east spouting their morals. They were individuals who knew both sides of the issue and chose to write what they saw and felt.

*...here we celebrated the 4th, I gave the men too much alcohol for peace, took a pretty hearty spree myself...*

Nathaniel Wyeth (7)

The manufacture and distribution of alcohol was big business at this time. (8) Many trappers changed their profession when the beaver trade declined, and the liquor market drew a few of them. Its production became such a problem between the Mexican territory and the American government that both sides were trying to control it.

The Taos Lightening that they made was a forbidden trade item with the Indian tribes and was one that the American government sought to control for the whites. While the northern government made inroads to help the situation manufactured in the states, the loss of drinkables was then filled in from the Santa Fe/Taos area.

*...we had a long talk with Mr. Mitchell about the abuse of selling whiskey to the Indians, whereby they become bad, dissolute, lazy and therefore dangerous. They omit, because of this, to sell good furs and merchandise to the Whites. The women, who know quite well that they profit nothing from their labor since the men barter them for whiskey...tan the skins only half way and badly.*

Prince Maximilian (9)

The El Pueblo and Hardscrabble settlements, just north of the Arkansas border, were major players in selling and distributing alcohol.

Many individuals like George Catlin (10) sat at McKenzie's tables in the American Fur Company's forts and drank Madeira and excellent ports with ice every day. William Fairholme was one of many who wrote about his drinks on the steam ships coming and going along the Missouri.

*In fact, all business in the States is carried on over a glass of mint julep, or sherry cobbler.*

William Fairholme (11)

*...drank a glass of grog to the health of our glorious old [George] Washington, this being his birthday.*

Francis Chardon (12)

Even the fair Susan Magoffin recorded in her journal what they drank. Simeon Turley is the most noted when talking about the manufacture of liquor south of the border, but he was not the only one to do it. Turley sent about $1500 -1700 a year back to the states each year from white trappers who exchanged their catches for the liquid. His "Taos Lightning" was a wheat-based whisky that was transported as far north as Fort Laramie over the old La Veta pass. Carried in small flat oak kegs on the back of mules, it was then diluted when close to the destination. LeRoy Hafen wrote these kegs could also be hidden in flour barrels and other larger containers. (13) There was another Kentuckian who did the same on a smaller scale.

*The quantity of wines and aguardiente produced by the vineyards and distilleries at and near Los Angeles, must be considerable – basing my estimate upon the statement of Mr. Wolfskil, an American gentleman residing here, and whose house and vineyard I visited. Mr. W.'s vineyard is young and covers about forty acres of ground, the number of vines being 4,000 or 5,000. From the purchase of these, he told me, that last year he made 180 casks of wine and the same quantity of aguardiente... The aguardiente and peach brandy, which I tasted, of his manufacture, being mellowed by age, were of an excellent flavor. The quantity of the wine and agudinete produced in California, I would suppose, amounted to 100,000 casks of sixteen gallons, or 1,600,000 gallons.*

Edwin Bryant (14)

Not all of it was the quality which we have today. George Brewerton (15) had an offer to join a man in some Monongahela (corn whiskey) while in Taos, *which it has ever been my misfortune to taste,* but was afraid of courtesy to

Turley's Mill: Portion of rock wall remains.

say no to. *"A large hole in my manners"* as he said.

What else do we know about alcoholic beverages in the fur trade era? The retail price of this liquid was pretty high. James Clyman wrote that the liquors at Fort Laramie were *"exorbitantly high"*. (16)

Note that the 2 pints Russell bought was more than what one of today's standard "fifths" contain, and would be enough for a several good drunks, if it wasn't watered down too much. For some reason, Russell was only charged half the regular price of $3 a pint. He also bought a considerable quantity of sugar. The accounts indicate that often the men would buy sugar and liquor together. Ashley's (17) account from the July 1825 Rendezvous shows a Gallon of Rum purchased by Mes. Gardner and Williams: 10 gallons rum – at $10 per gallon for a value of $100!

> *In my small outfit I had about five gallons of alcohol, in two kegs of three and two gallons, neatly packed in the bales of goods...*
>
> Charles Larpenteur (18)

> *It is very much to be regretted that at times like the present,* there should be a positive *necessity to allow the men as much rum as they can drink, but this course has been sanctioned and practiced by all leaders of parties who have hitherto visited these regions, and reform cannot be thought of now. The principle liquor in use here is alcohol diluted with water. It is sold to the men at three dollars a pint!*
>
> John Townsend (19)

The liquor trade was kept somewhat in control by our government, which even sent men to the west unannounced to catch the makers and sellers. Government inspectors were placed at Fort Leavenworth, Belleview, Westport and some other places to enforce these rules. Andrew Drips was one of these men sent west, but his trip and its purpose were leaked out beforehand so he never could accomplish much since they knew he was coming and could hide all the evidence.

A small amount of liquor was allowed on each shipment west for the men of the company to consume themselves. The law allowed for the companies to have one gill per man per day in their possession. (20) I don't think the government was against the use and selling of hard drinks in the early west. But there was a feeling that some control was needed, since it was abused by some for profit and was having a detestable effect among the western tribes. Furthermore, the government was not collecting any taxes on the sale of it like they did with other trade goods. So their control and oversight was not far behind. A bond had to be posted by each company trading in the west saying they would not sell, barter, exchange, or give liquor to the Indians. (21)

*My being a sober man was not much to my advantage, keeping me constantly in the liquor trade, and out of the charge of posts which some of my fellow-clerks took charge of, while I did all the work, and was really in charge when they got dead drunk.*
Charles Larpenteur (22)

*...however no one got drunk, yet we had wine, about two whole glasses each.*
Francis Ermatinger (23)

*...at noon partook of our national dinner, which was relished the better as we had a small portion of good old brandy, which we drank in a few minutes, deeply regretting that we had not a small portion of what was that day destroyed by the millions of freemen in the States...*
Zenas Leonard (24)

The sale of these liquids was such a secret that a code word was used for its sale in David Adam's journal, where he labeled it "milk." So, he could still account for the sale to his bosses, but not disclose what it really was.

David Adams' 1841-3 account books:
> *Pt mint milk*     $1.00
> *Sugar pint*      $2.00 (25)

The trade was deemed such a problem that as early as 1844, we find temperance unions in the newly settled Northwest.

*...here can be seen the great and salatory effects of temperance the judge*

Unknown people at an undetermined place showing the effects of a few drinks.

*the sheriff and several of the jurors having left the states, their friend's society and civilization on the account of the demoralizing effects of spirituous liquor here where no alcahall can be obtained…*

James Clyman (26)

There is another side of this that we often overlook, the use of alcohol beverages as medicine:

*One of our company named Ferguson, was bitten by a rattle-snake. We gave him rattlesnake's master and a quart of whisky, which seemed to have little or no effect as to producing inebriation, but soon relieved the pain of the bite, and the man rapidly recovered.*

Jacob Robinson (27)

The bottles were sometimes as important as what was in it and the people practiced "recycling" of them at this time. This was not the same as the Shrub which some journal writers mention and which Susan Magoffin liked. Eliza Smith gives us here version of how to make this refreshing drink:

*"Take two quarts of brandy, and put it in a large bottle, adding to it the juice of five lemons, the peels of two, and half a nutmeg; stop it up and let it stand three days, and add to it three pints of white wine, a pound and a half of sugar; mix it, strain it twice through a flannel, and bottle it up; it is a pretty wine, and a cordial."* (28)

### Drinks found in journals:

Monongahela (Corn) Whiskey
Taos lightning (wheat based)
White Lion Cocktail

| Pass Brandy | Mint Julep |
| Sherry cobbler | Port wines |
| Brandy | Gin cocktail |
| Hailstorms | Shrub |
| Malaga Wine | Aquadiente |

For all who do partake, here is a historical toast: *"Here's luck!"*

1. George Ruxton, *Ruxton of the Rockies*, LeRoy Hafen editor, University of Oklahoma Press, Norman, 1982, page 219.
2. Kenneth Holmes, *Ewing Young*, Abinfords and Mort Publishing, Portland Oregon, 1967, p 117.
3. William Fairholm, *Journal of an Expedition to the Grand Prairies of the Missouri*, Arthur Clark, Spokane, 1996, page 79.
4. David Brown, *Three Years in the Rocky Mountains*, Ye Galleon Press, Fairfield, 1982, pages 19, 20.
5. George Ruxton, *Life in the Far West*, LeRoy Hafen editor, University of Oklahoma Press, Norman, 1985, page 74.
6. Rufus Sage, *Rocky Mountain Life*, University of Nebraska Press, Lincoln, 1982, pages 52-3.
7. Nathaniel Wyeth, *The Journals of Captain Nathaniel J. Wyeth's Expeditions to the Oregon Country, 1831-1836*, Ye Galleon Press, Fairfield, 1997, page 75.

Foods of the Early American West

8. David Webber, *Taos Trappers, Taos Trappers,* University of Oklahoma, Norman, 1968, page 226.
9. Prince Maximilian, *People of the First Man,* Davis Thomas & Karin Ronnefeldt editors, Promontory Press, New York, 1982, page 107.
10. George Catlin, *Letters and Notes on the North American* Indians, JG Press, North Dighton, 1995, page 24.
11. Fairholm, page 50.
12. Francis Chardon, *Chardon's Journal at Fort Clark, 1834-1839,* University of Nebraska Press, Lincoln, 1997, page 59.
13. Leroy Hafen, *Fur Trade of the Far West,* University of Nebraska Press, Lincoln, 1986, volume 3, page 153.
14. Edwin Bryant, *Rocky Mountain Adventures,* Ye Galleon Press, Fairfield, 2000, page 412.
15. George Brewerton, *Overland with Kit Carson,* University of Nebraska, Lincoln, 1993, page 185.
16. James Clyman, *Journal of a Mountain* Man, Mountain Press Publishing, 1984, page 72
17. Dale Morgan, *The West of William H. Ashley,* Old West Publishing Company, Denver, Colorado, 1964, pages 127 & 8.
18. Charles Larpenteur, *Forty Years a Fur Trader on the Upper Missouri,* University of Nebraska Press, Lincoln, 1989, page 159.
19. John Townsend, *Across the Rockies to the Columbia,* University of Nebraska Press, Lincoln, 1978, page 83.
20. Catlin, page 24.
21. *President's Report on the Fur Trade,* Ye Galleon Press, Fairfield, 1985, page 44.
22. Larpenteur, page 137.
23. Francis Ermatinger, *The Fur Trade Letters of Francis Ermatinger,* Lois Halliday McDonald, Arthur Clark Company, Glendale, 1980, page 95.
24. Zenas Leonard, *Adventures of a Mountain Man,* Milo Quaife editor, University of Nebraska Press, Lincoln, 1978, pages 216-7.
25. David Adams, *The David Adam's Journals,* Charles Hanson, Jr. editor, Museum of the Fur Trade, Chadron, 1994, page 3.
26. Clyman, pages 159-60.
27. Jacob Robinson, *The Journal of the Santa Fe Expedition,* Narrative Press, Santa Barbara, 2001, page 2.
28. Eliza Smith, *Housewife, The Compleat Housewife,* published in 1748, Studio Editions facsimile edition, page 240.

# *Fruit and Honey*

*Here our leader halted, and then advanced quietly to a low bush, on top of which I perceived a piece of honey-comb. This I found was the bait or lure for the wild bees. Several were humming about it ... when they had laden themselves with honey, they would rise into the air and dart off in a straight line...in this way they trailed the honey laden bees to their hive...*

Washington Irving (1)

**I**RVING goes on in his journal to tell us that they followed the bees to their nest, axed the tree down and then brought a smoking fire into it to drive the bees out so they could rob the hive of its rich spoils. Spoons and knives were used to remove the sweetness, and the honey was placed in camp kettles for them to carry away. The remains were then left for other animals that also loved the honey and would finish the job.

We never think of sweet foods when we consider the staples of the frontier west, but the men and women who lived in it did. There are few natural sweet articles that fill this niche in their diets. Honey is the first we will mention here, but not the last.

*Here [Council Grove] we got some honey from the Indians, which was the first I tasted since I left Missouri.*

Joseph Williams (2)

Many wild fruits also had a sweet and/or tart taste to them which all races and nationalities liked. Descriptions of different bushes and trees that had sweet berries on them appear in the journals, and here are a few of the entries:

*There were black, white, yellow and red currants, large as cherries; though to the taste, quite inferior to the common garden currants, being less sweet, and more acid; plump gooseberries of a large size, likewise tempted the eye, but were equally sour. The bushes that bear them, frequently attain the height of eight or ten feet, in the rich mellow soil along the rivers; and at this season, are bent to the ground by the loads of fruit, with which they are encumbered. There was also a species of small tree, not unlike the hawthorn, armed with thorns, and covered with blue or lead colored leaves, which was completely enveloped with berries, either red or yellow, about the size of allspice or pepper grains. This fruit is extremely sour, and is commonly called "buffalo berries."*

Warren Ferris (3)

*Upon all the principal streams were large quantities of cherries and plums which proved quite acceptable. The cherry (cerasus virgina) indigenous to this country is quite similar in appearance to our common wild cherry, though it is generally larger and more pleasantly tasted. It grows upon a small bush and yields lavish profusion.*

Rufus Sage (4)

*Here again I displayed my genius for culinary invention, for I determined to have a second course to our dinner; and after each of the party had brought his hat and pockets full of plums, I selected some of the ripest and bruised them in one of our pots, added sugar and a little water and upon this great excitement we agreed to lavish a glass of our remaining half bottle of brandy, which we threw in, and allowed the whole to simmer over the fire for a quarter of a hour. But what name this strange mess should be called, I know not; but whether pudding, tart or stewed plums, we voted it excellent, although there was still left in it acid and bitter enough to make any English school boy draw up the corners of his mouth and eyes and vote it excellent.*

Charles Murray (5)

James Clyman in his journal tells us he guarded a group of women and young ones who gathered wild currants and choke cherries that grew in the area they were camped in. He noted that the cherries found there were of the finest kind. (6)

> *At a short distance from camp, the men get great quantities of very fine plums.*
>
> George Sibley (7)

Francis Chardon writes while he was a clerk at Fort Clark, small groups that went searching for berries, plums and cherries in September and October, his first year at the fort. (8)

Susan Magoffin also comments that grapes and plums which were not ripe when she came through; but were all along the little streams they passed, so it was something they looked for and noticed. (9) Jacob Fowler and some of his men were picking grapes when a bear attacked the trapping group. (10)

> *On entering [a friend's lodge], we were shown seats on robes, and as it was about their breakfast time, we were asked to eat, but declined. They insisted we should take some honey; and a wooden bowl, or deep trencher filled with honey and part of a buffalo horn so shaped that it could be used as a spoon, was set before us. And we enjoyed the feast, passing the spoon back and forth, Indian fashion. He brought out a raw hide bag full of honey, and after warming it by the fire and kneading it occasionally, succeeded in filling the pail as full as we could conveniently carry it on horseback to camp at Big John Creek.*
>
> James Webb (11)

> *...we have 3 kinds of currants, one of gooseberry all different from those of*

# Foods of the Early American West

*the U.S. and Service berrys all the first were sour, the latter sweet.*

Nathaniel Wyeth (12)

*We found a considerable quantity of a small fruit called the chock-cherry, a species of the prunus growing on low bushes. When ripe, they are tolerable eating, somewhat astringent, however, producing upon the mouth the same effect, though in a less degree, as he unripe persimmon. They are now generally green, or we should feast luxuriantly upon them.*

John Townsend (13)

*The narrow bottoms along it were occasionally covered with bushes bearing a delicious fruit called service berries, by the American hunters, and pears (Des Poires) by the Canadians; a species of black hawthorn berries, wild currents, goose berries, black cherries, and buffalo cherries were also at intervals abundant.*

Warren Ferris (14)

*In the following the course of the stream on which we encamped last night, found cherries in abundance, had time to stop and gather as we wished. In deed, we rambled until noon, before we went into camp. The cherries are very fine equal to any we find in the states.*

Narcissa Whitman (15)

*Nothing remarkable happened en route which had not been presented in previous descriptions, except that we found a great abundance of fruit of the berry variety. The largest of the berries we saw was scarcely as big as our little wood cherries. The cherries were in clusters like our cherries. The pears were in clusters like our cherries. The billberries, more tasty than our own, are also more pleasing to the eye. They were of a brilliant violet color, like the red of a currant. Another fruit that resembles it, and which is called the buffalo berry because the animals are very fond of it, was more abundant than all of the others.*

Nicholas Point (16)

*Raisins, a different kind of sweet, were listed as a trade item for the 1827 rendezvous. The price of these (shown below) was the cost of Smith, Jackson and Sublette, the retail price being higher than that. **"Mountain prices"** or what the price was to be sold at was usually 100 to 150 % higher than the cost of the goods.*
*Raisins at one dollar fifty cents per pound…*

William Ashley (17)

*At a short distance from camp, the men got great quantities of very fine plums...*

George Sibley (18)

*...picked fine strawberries...*

James Clyman (19)

*I still found in my food bag a little rice, whereof we cooked ourselves a thin soup. The other empty spaces in our stomachs we filled with wild currants and bullberries that grew along the shores. The latter, also called rabbit berries, are the fruit of the Shepardia argentea, a large bush, whose leaves are shiny white on the under side. The red berries in appearance and taste resemble currants were still unripe. Nevertheless they tasted famously.*

Fredrick Wislizenus (20)

By all these entries, we see that all species of natural sweets and berries were used and relished when they were found in season and then relished. Many of you will not read of these entries in any other book. This food group makes up not only another section of the food chain, but an aid in the health and diet of the people. Berries not only taste different than meat or other staples, they feel different to the mouth. It is interesting to note that some of the "extras" to the inhabitant's yearly diets are found in the fall, which works well for them to stockpile or consume before the winter drains the body.

If you are like me, enjoy sweets, in all of its forms. Evidently, the first whites west and those who grew up here did the same.

1.  Washington Irving, *A Tour on the Prairies*, University of Oklahoma Press, Norman, 1971, pages 51-3.
2.  Joseph Williams, *Narrative of a Tour from the State of Indiana to the Oregon Territory in the Years 1841-2*, Ye Galleon Press, Fairfield, 1977, pages 57-8.
3.  Warren Ferris, *Life in the Rocky Mountains*, Old West Publishing, Denver, 1983, pages 341-2.
4.  Rufus Sage, *Rocky Mountain Life*, University of Nebraska Press, Lincoln, 1982, page 344.
5.  Charles Murray, *Travels in North America*, William Blackwood and Sons, London, 1900, page 319.
6.  James Clyman, *Journal of a Mountain* Man, Mountain Press Publishing, Missoula, 1984, page 97.
7.  George Sibley, *The Road to Santa Fe*, Kate Gregg editor, University of New Mexico Press, Albuquerque, 1968, page 68.

8.  Francis Chardon, *Chardon's Journal at Fort Clark, 1834-1839*, University of Nebraska Press, Lincoln, 1997, page 7.
9.  Susan Magoffin, *Down the Santa Fe Trail and into Mexico*, Stella Drumm, editor, Yale University Press, New Haven, 1962, pages 36-7.
10. Jacob Fowler, *The Journal of Jacob Fowler*, Elliot Coues editor, Ross & Haines, Inc., Minneapolis, 1965, page 41.
11. James Webb, *Adventures in the Santa Fe Trade 1844-1847*, Ralph Bieber editor, University of Nebraska, Lincoln, 1995, page 168.
12. Nathaniel Wyeth, *The Journals of Captain Nathaniel J. Wyeth's Expeditions to the Oregon Country, 1831-1836*, Ye Galleon Press, Fairfield, 1997, page 16.
13. John Townsend, *Across the Rockies to the Columbia*, University of Nebraska Press, Lincoln, 1978, page 249.
14. Ferris, page 128.
15. *Narcissa Whitman, My Journal*, University of Nebraska Press, Lincoln, 1989, page 38.
16. Nicholas Point, *Wilderness Kingdom*, Loyola Press, Chicago, 1967, page 188.
17. Dale Morgan, *The West of William H. Ashley*, Old West Publishing Company, Denver, Colorado, 1964, page 151.
18. Sibley, page 68.
19. Clyman, page 72.
20. Dr. Fredrick Wislizenus, *A Journey to the Rocky Mountains in the Year 1839*, Ye Galleon Press, Fairfield, 1989, page 132.

An essential spice.

# Spices

*...soon struck a branch of the Salt Fork... the banks of which were composed of large salt rocks, from which the men broke off large pieces with their tomahawks. Here, and in the Salt River was enough of this valuable mineral to supply the world for an indefinite period.*

Thomas James (1)

**W**HAT can be added to any food that improves the taste, can sometimes preserve it and change the taste without a change in the method of cooking? Spices – another of the items associated with cooking and food that you use probably everyday in your modern kitchen but we just don't hear much about in history books. This chapter will enlighten you more on the subject.

# Foods of the Early American West

*On the eighth, I set out with others to procure salt, at a place discovered by our hunters yesterday. We passed three miles down the river, and found the salt in a slough on the west side of it. It was found on the surface of a black stinking mire, fifty or sixty paces in circuit; the upper strata was fine, and white as snow, to the depth of two inches; beneath which, was a layer of beautiful crystals, to the depth of five or six inches, that rested on the surface of the mire. We slowly sank into the latter to our knees, whilst scooping up the salt, and then changed places, for we could scarcely extricate ourselves at that depth; and concluded that if we should remain long enough in the same spot, we would at length disappear entirely.*

Warren Ferris (2)

Spices of all kinds were found in the west and used commonly. Some were used in castor bait recipes to draw in beaver to the traps. Spices are also found in estate records, inventory lists, sold at rendezvous and were in almost every log and adobe home on the frontier.

Mustard, cream of tartar, calomel, nutmeg and camphor are found in James Baird's estate. (3) In William Ashley's journal we also see allspice, agreed upon to be provided as a resalable item. It was to be purchased at $1.50 per pound. (4) As a trade good at the rendezvous, pepper was going for the high price of $6.00 a pound. Compare that price with what they were charging for sugar – $2.00 a pound. (5) Sometimes food only had salt or pepper applied to it.

*Presenting a surface of sand the most beautiful Salt was found in many places and within two or three inches of the surface. I ascertained that although the salt was found in a Layer it did not extend throughout the plain. In passing the plain pieces of the salt were frequently thrown out by the feet of the horses. The Layer was about 3/4 of an inch thick and when the sand was removed from it I found the salt pure white with a grain as fine as table salt.*

Jedediah Smith (6)

*The extravagant use of red pepper among the Mexicans has become truly proverbial. It enters into nearly every dish at every meal, and often so predominates as entirely to conceal the character of the viands. It is likewise ground into a sauce, and thus used even more abundantly than butter. Chile verde (green pepper), not as a mere condiment, but as a salad, served up in different ways, is reckoned by them one of the greatest luxuries.*

Josiah Gregg (7)

*Next day's march brought us to Sweet-Water River, which rises in the southeastern extremity of the Wind Mountains, and flows eastward one hundred and*

*fifty miles, falling into the Platte, a few miles above the Red Hills. This river owes its name to the accidental drowning in it of a mule loaded with sugar, some years since...*
Warren Ferris (8)

*Major Biddle experienced a severe attack of cramp in the stomach, but soon found relief from swallowing a quantity of ginger, the only medicine with which they were provided.*
Stephen Long (9)

*He* [a young Arikara] *had brought with him from one of the upper branches of that river* [Arkansa] *two masses of salt, each weighing about thirty pounds. This salt is pure and perfect, consisting of large crystalline grains, so concentrated together to form a mass about twenty inches in diameter and six in thickness.*
Stephen Long (10)

The entries shown here only touch the surface of what was really used to "spice" up all the foods in the west. This is a topic that when talking about food overlaps with other similar ones. Another chapter will look further into the hot spicy ingredients that were found in the Hispanic foods and other ethnic foods.

1. Thomas James, *Three Years Among the Indians and Mexicans*, Milo Quaife editor, Citadel Press, New York, 1966, page 121.
2. Warren Ferris, *Life in the Rocky Mountains*, Old West Publishing, Denver, 1983, page 346.
3. LeRoy Hafen, *The Fur Trade of the Far West*, Spokane, Arthur Clark Company, Denver, 1965, volume 3, pages 36-7.
4. Dale Morgan, *The West of William H. Ashley*, Old West Publishing Company, Denver, Colorado, 1964, page 151.
5. Morgan, page 168.
6. Jedediah Smith, *A Southwest Expedition of Jedediah Smith*, University of Nebraska Press, Lincoln, 1989, page 89.
7. Josiah Gregg, *Commerce of the Prairies*, Milo Milton Quaife editor, University of Nebraska Press, Lincoln, 1967, page 147.
8. Warren Ferris, *Life in the Rocky Mountains*, Old West Publishing, Denver, 1983, pages 109-110.
9. Maxine Benson, *From Pittsburg to the Rocky Mountains, Major Stephen Long's Expedition 1819-1820*, Fulcrum Books, Golden Colorado, 1988, page 75.
10. Benson, page 165.

# Desserts

*The first class gourmets – that is the factors at the forts, the traders and the bigwigs of the forts and trading posts – crown their repasts with a dish of beef berries mixed with cream and sugar. But the Indians' taste is simpler.*

Nicholas Point (1)

**S**OME may consider this topic as being better placed as the last chapter in the book, since desserts are usually at the end to any modern meal. But those who know me have seen that I partake of desserts at a different time in the order of the meal (at the first) and so it is placed here – in a very historic manner as Father Nicholas Point does.

*The only seasoning they know is a good appetite and when there is dessert, they have it first as we do soup, or as wine was drunk in olden times.*

Nicholas Point (2)

Not many historians speak or write much on the sweet endings to meals, but as you have seen here so far, and will see more of, desserts were popular, but limited in range.

> *Coffee and chocolate are cooked…*
>
> Fredrick Wislizenus (3)

Here are a few entries on the pleasant foods:

> *We had a fine dinner today and I enjoyed it exceedingly, for I had eaten nothing but a little tea and half a biscuit since yesterday dinner. It consisted of boiled chicken, soup, rice and a dessert made of wine and gooseberry tart. Such a thing on the plains would be looked upon by those at home as an utter impossibility. But nevertheless it is true.*
>
> Susan Magoffin (4)

Lewis Garrard, when trying to convey how badly they wanted good, pure water on a section of the trail, writes that his group had to use a half full keg of salty water to make their coffee. Then, while they were heading to Bent's Fort, they met a man on foot, under the hot sun which was wilting them, carrying a canteen. He noted that the canteen filled with molasses, which had cost two dollars, he was willing to give it for just one drink of water. They had none themselves, so the man just walked on, with no exchange happening. (5)

Molasses may seem out of place here in the Rocky Mountains, but Joseph Williams saw and recorded how it was made by one group:

> *I went out to see them making molasses from their small corn stalks. They ground them, and then pressed out the juice, which they boiled into molasses. (6)*

Missionary wife Mary Walker wrote in her diary about her son Marcus' five-years-old birthday celebration:

> *Mr. E's [Edward's] boys came by to eat cake & ice cream with ours. (7)*

William Gilpin's account of a special 4th of July celebration at Fort St. Vrain in 1843 also notes sweet stuffs they enjoyed with Colonel Fremont, Fremont's men and the fort's employees:

> *They raised the flag, fired a salute from Fremont's howitzer, and served cake and ice cream. The fruit cake had been made by Senator Benton's niece at St. Louis, milk came from the goats at the fort and snow for the freezing from Long's Peak. (8)*

How out of place is that? It should also be noted that reports say they had buffalo steaks and macaroni along with the fruit cake and ice cream at that celebration!

I am sure a few of you are waiting for me to show the use of chocolate; it was found mainly in the southwest and was a much coarser and darker mixture than we have today. But it must have been just as good, as it was well received by those in the region.

*...no one can hesitate to do homage to their incomparable chocolate, in the preparation of which the Mexicans surely do excel every other people.*

Josiah Gregg (9)

*I was somewhat amused today by observing one of our newly hired men enter the tent and order, with the air of a man who knew he would not be refused, twenty dollars of rum, and ten dollars worth of sugar, to treat two of his companions who were leaving the rendezvous!*

John Townsend (10)

While all this sounds great to us, one mountaineer would disagree:

*The voyager is never more satisfied then when he has a good supply of buffalo-beef at his command. It is then, his greasy visage bespeaks content, and his jocund voice and merry laugh evinces the deep-felt pleasure and gratification that reign within.*

*Talk not to him of the delicacies of civilized life, - of pies, puddings, soups, fricassees, roast beef, pound cake and dessert – he cares for none of these things, and will laugh at your verdancy!*

*He knows his own reference, and will tell you your boasted excellencies are not to be compared with it. If you object to the sameness of his simple fare, he will recount the several varieties of its parts, and descant upon each of their peculiar merits. He will illustrate the numerous and dissimilar modes of so preparing them, that they cannot fail to excite by their presence and appease by their taste the appetite of the most fastidious. And then in point of health, there is nothing equal to buffalo-meat. It alone, will cure dyspepsy, prevent consumption, amend a broken constitution, put flesh upon the bones of a skeleton and restore a dead man again to life!*

Rufus Sage (11)

Well, this is probably the only time I won't agree with Rufus Sage on any topic, but as noted here, desserts were found in the time frame and in the west. So, enjoy!

1.  Nicholas Point, *Wilderness Kingdom*, Loyola Press, Chicago, 1967, page 129.
2.  Point, page 129.
3.  Dr. Fredrick Wislizenus, *A Journey to the Rocky Mountains in the Year 1839*, Ye Galleon Press, Fairfield, 1989, pages 87-8.
4.  Susan Magoffin, *Down the Santa Fe Trail and into Mexico*, Stella Drumm, editor, Yale University Press, New Haven, 1962, pages 36-7.
5.  Lewis Garrard, *Wah-to-yah and the Taos Trail*, University of Oklahoma Press, Norman, 1957, page 247.
6.  Joseph Williams, *Narrative of a Tour from the State of Indiana to the Oregon Territory in the Years 1841-2*, Ye Galleon Press, Fairfield, 1977, page 55.
7.  Clifford Drury, *On to Oregon*, University of Nebraska Press, Lincoln, 1998, page 312.
8.  Diane Brotemarkle, *Old Fort St. Vrain*, Self Published, Boulder, 2001, page 84.
9.  Josiah Gregg, *Commerce of the Prairies*, Milo Milton Quaife editor, University of Nebraska Press, Lincoln, 1967, page 147.
10. John Townsend, *Across the Rockies to the Columbia*, University of Nebraska Press, Lincoln, 1978, pages 83-4.
11. Rufus Sage, *Rocky Mountain Life*, University of Nebraska Press, Lincoln, 1982, page 69.

# Dried and Preserved Foods

*It is a rich sight indeed to look at the fine fat meat stretched out on ropes to dry for our sustenance when we are no longer in the regions of the living animal. Such soup as we have made of hump ribs, one of the most choice parts of the buffalo, I never ate its equal in the best hotels of N. Y. and Philadelphia.*

Susan Magoffin (1)

**S**INCE there was no dependable way of keeping meat fresh and edible for any length of time, or to preserve it, various methods were used to keep foodstuffs that could not be eaten quickly. Food storage needed attention, despite what William Anderson wrote in his diary:

*Never was there a purer, drier or more elastic atmosphere than we have breathed and enjoyed the last thirty days. I have not seen, or smelt a piece of meat approaching to putrefaction, since I reached the Platte. Except for the heart of man, I believe meat would petrify before it would putrify. (2)*

In the cold winter months, food spoilage was not a problem, but for rest of the year, when warmer, it could be. And to have worked hard to obtain food, and then allow it to spoil, did not set well with the tribes of Native

Americans or any other ethnic group.

We see two ways largely practiced by the Native tribes – smoking and drying. They may seem like the same process, but they are not. Both use some form of rack to hang the meat. Drying can be done without the use of a fire or the smoke that comes from it, and relies on the sun or a slight wind to help in this method. Smoking is done with a small, low fire and plenty of rotten or wet wood or leaves.

Reginald Laubin (3) in his Indian tipi book shows how the dried meat was cut, by slicing a big roast very thin, in as long a continuous piece as you can, like you were unrolling it. This strip is a much larger and longer one than many of us today use when smoking or drying. Instead of the small bits and pieces we usually see smoked today, he describes meat sections maybe a hand's width wide and a foot to a foot and half long. This size of meat would hang better on the racks. It was more practical, not only in the effort needed to do it, but in serving sizes. Remember, these people were not putting their meat in small cloth sacks, but large rawhide parfleches.

*All we found in stock at this time was dried buffalo meat, of which we took a supply with us.*

Fredrick Wislizenus (4)

Many of the caravans and small groups going west invested in dried meat as one of the staples they carried with them.

*At our noon encampment we commenced the process of "making meat," preparatory to passing a long distance devoid of game; and, as the reader may be anxious to know what kind of an operation this is, I will explain. It consists simply in cutting into thin slices the boneless parts of buffalo, or other meat, and drying them in the wind or sun. Meat thus cured may be preserved for years without salt. Ropes of raw hide were stretched around the wagons, upon which the results of our labor were left to the finishing effects of the wind and sun as we proceeded, —thus making an important saving in the item of time. It is astonishing how long a time fresh meat may be kept without injury, upon the grand prairies, in dry weather, when it receives the free access of air. Some of that killed on our first arrival among buffalo was yet hanging to the wagons, as sweet and sound as ever. I have known it to be preserved, in this way, for ten or twelve days in the heat of summer. Meat, packed in snow, while in a frozen state, may be retained fresh for months without injury.*

Rufus Sage (5)

Preserving meat was something that all groups needed. To show just how important preserving of meat was to the everyday life of every

An ancient way to store foods.

individual, you are going to read a lengthy set of journal and dairy lines on this and how often it was done. Jedediah Smith, David Jackson and William Sublette entered into an agreement to purchase from William Ashley this food stuff on July 18th, 1826 - dried fruit at $1.50 a pound, which they would then resell at the rendezvous. (6)

> *...traded for 18 horses and 600 lbs dried salmon which I had reserved for provisions after we leave the river...*

Nathaniel Wyeth (7)

> *...we remained in camp all day to "make meat", which is done by cutting it in thin slices and putting it on scaffolds over the fire to dry, then it is packed in bales formed of hard dressed leather, called "par fleche"...*

James Abert (8)

> *Octr 20th a Village of Bonnaks [sp] consisting of 250 Lodges arrived at the Fort from these we traded a considerable quantity of furs, and a large supply of dried meat.*

Osborne Russell (9)

> *Fresh meat is now very grateful to our palates, as we have been living for weeks past on nothing by poor, dried buffalo, the better, and far the larger part, having been deposited in the fort for the subsistence of the men who remain. We have no flour, nor vegetables of any kind, and our meat may be aptly compared to dry chips, breaking short off in our fingers; and when boiled to softened it a little, and render it for mastication, not a star appears in our pot. It seems astonishing that life can be sustained upon such miserable fare, and yet our men (except when under the influence of liquor) have never murmured, but have always eaten their*

*crusty meal and drunk their cold water with light and excellent spirits. We hope soon to fall in with the buffalo...*

John Townsend (10)

Everyone has heard of Pemmican, but most do not know how it was made and put into parfleches which were sometimes then buried. To me, this is definitely a survival food. Everyone had their own recipe for the package, to be served at a later meal, and each was based on the local foods available.

*Sometime after they were gone I went to a bale of dried meat which had been spread in the sun...*

Osborne Russell (11)

One preserved food that we think of as purely American is bacon. This pork product was preserved, usually by salting. Bacon shows up with Jacob Fowler (12) when it was brought out after being hidden in his packs for six months. How did he do that and why? It was a special occasion and he needed something to pleasantly surprise the men with. But that is not the only time we see it.

George Sibley lists as part of the food supplies he had purchased for the group when surveying the Santa Fe Trail, one box that weighed 400 pounds of commercially dried meat. (13)

Phillip Covington while on his western trip noted they ate a side of bacon, fresh pork and potatoes until they reached the imaginary "buffalo hunting" line. (14)

*...We were invited to the back part of the lodge, where dried, pounded cherries, mixed with buffalo marrow and a root, eaten raw resembling in taste and appearance the Jerusalem artichoke were set before us...*

Lewis Garrard (15)

*The manner of grinding corn is also worthy of notice. Five or six women sit behind as many hoppers, each of which is composed of a curved rock, placed in a box. Each woman holds in her hand a rough stone, about 1 inch long, and three or four inches in diameter; with one hand she occasionally throws corn upon the large rock, which she rubs with the smaller stone until the corn becomes meal. An equal number of women sit in front of the hoppers, singing a wild Indian song, by the notes of which the mills keep regular time in grinding. It is a very quick method, and I think preferable to gritting, which is frequently practiced in the west.*

Jacob S. Robinson (16)

> *...if the journey goes through a region where neither buffalo nor other game is to be found, the buffalo meat is dried as follows: the meat is cut in strips as thin as possible, and hung upon poles or scaffold, and there allowed to dry in the sun. If time is limited, a little fire is at first maintained under it; but it tastes better without the fire. When it is dried, it is beaten with a stone or hammer to make it more tender. It is then eatable, either dry or cooked, and can be kept for years, if protected against moisture and insects. The so-called toro is still more suitable for preservation. For its preparation this dried meat is beaten with a stone into a coarse grained powder, and mixed with as much melted buffalo fat and tallow as will hold. The paste thus formed is pressed as compactly as possible into a bag of buffalo skin, which is then firmly sewed up.*

Fredrick Wislizenus (17)

As you can see, this skill was known by every person, no matter their status, race or class. It was an important section of the food items that kept families and groups alive through lean times, and used when a quick meal had to be done with little around to make it or while in the saddle and no time was made to stop, make a fire and prepare a meal.

Preserved foods were a great source of relief for western traveler. It did not have to be cooked, was impervious to most weather conditions for short periods of time and when game was not available, was the only source of food handy. No wonder it is found so often in every well planned camp or home.

1.  Susan Magoffin, , *Down the Santa Fe Trail and into Mexico*, Stella Drumm, editor, Yale University Press, New Haven, 1962, page 43.
2.  William Anderson, *The Rocky Mountain Journals of William Marshall Anderson*, University of Nebraska Press, Lincoln, 1987, page 129.
3.  Reginald Laubin, *The Indian Tipi*, Stanley Vestal editor, University of Oklahoma Press, Norman, 1977, page 150.
4.  Dr. Fredrick Wislizenus, *A Journey to the Rocky Mountains in the Year 1839*, Ye Galleon Press, Fairfield, 1989, pages 69-70.
5.  Rufus Sage, *Rocky Mountain Life*, University of Nebraska Press, Lincoln, 1982, page?
6.  Dale Morgan, *The West of William H. Ashley*, Old West Publishing Company, Denver, Colorado, 1964, page 151.
7.  Nathaniel Wyeth, *The Journals of Captain Nathaniel J. Wyeth's Expeditions to the Oregon Country, 1831-1836*, Ye Galleon Press, Fairfield, 1997, page 84.
8.  James Abert, *Expedition to the Southwest*, University of Nebraska Press, Lincoln, 1999, page 60.

9.   Osborne Russell, *Journal of a Trapper*, University of Nebraska Press, Lincoln, 1986, page 8.

10.  John Townsend, *Across the Rockies to the Columbia*, University of Nebraska Press, Lincoln, 1978, page 122.

11.  Russell, page 101.

12.  Jacob Fowler, *The Journal of Jacob Fowler*, Elliot Coues editor, Ross & Haines, Inc., Minneapolis, 1965, page 73.

13.  George Sibley, *The Road to Santa Fe*, Kate Gregg editor, University of New Mexico Press, Albuquerque, 1968, page 176.

14.  John Covington, *Colorado Magazine,* July, 1950 Colorado Historical Society.

15.  Lewis Garrard, *Wah-to-yah and the Taos Trail*, University of Oklahoma Press, Norman, 1957, page 48.

16.  Jacob S. Robinson, *Journal of the Santa Fe Expedition*, Narrative Press, Santa Barbara, 2001, page 22.

17.  Fredrick Wislizenus, *A Journey to the Rocky Mountains in the Year 1839*, Ye Galleon Press, Fairfield, 1989, page 52.

# Foods Popular on the Missouri Frontier

*There sat the Captain of the rangers and his officers, round a three legged table, crowned by a broad and smoking dish of boiled beef and turnips.*

Washington Irving (1)

THIS kind lady of the house then offered bread and butter to Irving, who exclaimed "what a banquet!" An interesting aspect of the early western travelers is that they stopped in and sometimes even stayed for short layovers at the small frontier cabins they found on the trails. These houses were the first and sometimes last scenes which reminded them of their homes and these hardy men did not find them repugnant to use or stay in. The housewives who lived and worked in them became a very eagerly looked forward to sight, because they usually had the first home cooked foods or the ingredients for the men to make their own meals, which they had not had for a very long time.

James Webb tells us about a time when he found himself and the men with him at a frontier cabin:

*I bought a ham that weighed about twenty pounds, four and a half dozen eggs, flour, potatoes and lard for shortening, sugar for our coffee, etc... We ate all the ham and eggs, and all of the other provisions we could hold. We went to the house to settle and they wanted to know if we could not get some buttermilk. The woman had just finished churning and we told to bring what she had. She brought a large white pitcher full – I think near a gallon – and we passed around the pitcher until emptied. We settled and rode off- riding slowly.*

James Webb (2)

*The first day's march conducted us through a fertile and cultivated tract of country, to the Missouri river, opposite St. Charles. We crossed the stream in a flat boat, and passing through the village, halted for the night at a farmhouse a few miles beyond. Corn and corn-stalks were purchased for our horses, and corn bread and bacon for ourselves.*

Warren Ferris (3)

This was not only true for the frontier home and the wayfaring men; the food they ate at the hotels and boarding houses while in St. Louis and Independence were recorded too. William Fairholme, when he arrived in St. Louis, stayed with six others in one large room. But the hotel did have three or four French cooks. (4) It was called "The Inn" at Burtonville. He also writes about using the "Table d'Hote" [dish of the day]. (5)

While these homes were looked forward to and welcomed, some of the items in them were found to be uncomfortable after many months of rustic travel. Lewis Garrard wrote:

*...our hands unconsciously found their way to the scalp knife at the waist band, and we laughed more than once at ourselves for using left hand fingers in lieu of*

*the awkward two-tined fork.* (6)

Silverware and tables and chairs were not the only things the mountaineers found different when they returned to the states: beds, closed up rooms and even sheets or table coverings seemed strange and foreign to them.

*...we halted that night in the village, where, in a house of a white farmer, I ate the first civilized meal I had tasted for many months, and enjoyed the unusual luxury of eating at a table with knife and fork; moreover sitting on a chair, which, however, I would gladly have dispensed with, for I had so long been accustomed to sit Indian fashion on the ground, that a chair was at first both unpleasant and awkward. The meal consisted of hoe cakes and honey, delicious butter and lettuce and radishes.*

George Ruxton (7)

Francis Parkman, like many of the more well-off travelers, kept records of his trip expenses. In his two volume set, gave a lot of information on his expenses while traveling. (8) He had in one example of breakfast while in a fairly nice place; 25 – 36 cents, a meal and tea were $1.00. (9) So what a tin cup of sugar or coffee cost in the west could buy you a very nice meal in a large East coast city.

*It* [the meal at a cabin] *consisted of pork chops, ham, eggs, Indian bread and butter, tea, coffee, milk, potatoes, preserved ginger, and though last, certainly not least in value, an enormous tin dish of plovers, (the contents of my game-bag,) fricasseed. Here was certainly a most abundant repast and we did ample justice to it.*

John Kirk Townsend (10)

> *To see men with boots and shoes on, to dine at a table, and to eat with forks again is a right pleasant thing – Who would have thought, 8 months ago, that such would be my thoughts at this time?*
>
> William Anderson (11)

These cabins, the friendly faces in them and warm meals really made the day for any weary travelers. We think of them sleeping under the stars, long ranging men to never have thought of, nor considered a cabin as a place to be at. But they did. History is like that: we tend to get myopic in our thoughts and feelings concerning this time frame by what we see on movies and in our general reading. It turns out that history can always be fresh and new to us.

1. Washington Irving, *A Tour of the Prairies*, University of Oklahoma Press, Norman, 1971, page 212.
2. James Webb, *Adventures in the Santa Fe Trade 1844-1847*, Ralph Bieber editor, University of Nebraska, Lincoln, 1995, page 122.

3.  Warren Angus Ferris, *Life in the Rocky Mountains*, Old West Publishing, Denver, 1983, page 82.
4.  William Fairholme, *Journal of an Expedition to the Grand Prairies of the Missouri*, Arthur Clark, Spokane, 1996, pages 49-50.
5.  Fairholme, page 60.
6.  Lewis Garrard, *Wah-to-yah and the Taos Trail*, University of Oklahoma Press, Norman, 1957, page 297.
7.  George Ruxton, *Ruxton of the Rockies*, LeRoy Hafen editor, University of Oklahoma Press, Norman, 1982, page 289.
8.  Francis Parkman, *The Journals of Francis Parkman*, Harper and Brothers, New York, 1947 (two volumes), pages 492 and on.
9.  Parkman, page 496.
10. John Kirk Townsend, *Across the Rockies to the Columbia*, University of Nebraska Lincoln, Press, 1978, page 1.
11. William Anderson, *The Rocky Mountain Journals of William Marshall Anderson*, University of Nebraska Press, Lincoln, 1987, page 209.

# Southwestern Foods

*On Mr. St. Vrain's table was the national dish – Chile Colorado – a compound of red-pepper pods and other spicy ingredients; a hot mess at first; but, with the aid of tortillas (a thin, soft cake of flour and water baked on a griddle) of which we consumed a great number – a new taste was soon acquired.*

Lewis Garrard (1)

**T**HE first whites who tasted southwestern dishes found them not only strange and unusual, but hard on their digestive systems. The spiciness of dishes not only tasted strong but gave them diarrhea which made horseback travel much more difficult. The situation was not so different than when travelers would switch to an all meat diet.

This does not mean it was considered to be awful food to them, for many came to love it and have it daily. It was just a total change from the bland servings they were used to, not only on the plains and intermountain region, but from what they ate in their original homes too.

# Foods of the Early American West

Mexican foods show up in all of the journals of the people who traveled there. Ruxton, Gregg and Garrard all give many lines on the food they had while in the southwest and west. Lewis Garrard even mentioned using beans instead of money for gambling, and noted the way that they changed hands, was a caution to a hungry man. (2) It was not only the well known foods, simple ingredients like chilies, tortillas or beans that are found in their books:

*...where the herders boarded and made cheese. The curd was prepared in the usual way with rennet, and set in small kettles and earthen water-vessels; and when in proper condition, tied in a cloth and pressed by placing it upon a flat rock and a heavy stone upon it. We were invited to eat of it and found it very good, for the time and place, but by any means what I was accustomed to eat as cheese at home.*

James Webb (3)

George Brewerton stayed at United States Hotel on the Plaza in Santa Fe where he had *chicken fixin's and corn doings*, and he could have had Frijoles and tortillas. He was worried that his trail worn clothes would not meet the standard for the table there, but he had nothing to worry about as all the rest of the diners had similar or worse clothes. (4)

These meals of "chicken and fixin's" were 50 cents a person. When dinner was ready, there was a mad dash by the renters wanting to fill that *"Aching void"* of hunger for good food. The furnishings mentioned were wooden benches, pine tables, earthen ware plates and ill made cutlery. Brewerton heard French, German, Spanish and different dialects of American when eating there.

Matthew Field sat down in a similar tavern and didn't even order any food, but had a filled plate put in front of him - *"seemed we must, if were hungry,"* whether they liked the dish or not. The host knew nothing about such a question as "What will you have?" either in Spanish or English. Field did like the dish and had seconds, with grapes, apples, other fruits and a glass of genuine Poteen or pass whiskey to wash it all down. (5)

The records of the food eaten in the Southwest are extensive; here are a few:

*To the house of Don Louis Rubideau... we were duly escorted, and after a delicious meal of roasted sheep ribs, eggs, wheaten cakes, and coffee, we spent the evening in satisfying the enquires of the Alacalde about St. Louis and all the friends he had left there.*

Matthew Field (6)

*In the corner of the hut we found a bucket of milk; so, sans ceremonie, it was hung over the fire with crumbled biscoche...*

Lewis Garrard (7)

*...they have large flocks of sheep and goats, to watch day and night. The milk and meat of the goats are part of their food, and they also make excellent cheese of the milk...*

Joseph Williams (8)

*They raise onions, peas, beans, corn, wheat and red pepper--the last a principal ingredient in Spanish food.*

Thomas James (9)

*The fare in Laforey's house was what might be expected in a hunter's establishment: venison, antelope and the meat of the carnero cimarron, the rocky mountain sheep, furnished his larder, and such meat (poor and tough at this season of the year) with cakes of Indians meal, either tortillas of gorditas.*

George Ruxton (10)

*We had been on short rations for two days... but I resolved to have a feast, and setting all hands to forage, on return we found our combined efforts had produced an imposing pile of several yards of beef, onions, chiles, frijoles, sweet corn, eggs & c. an enormous olla was procured and everything was bundled pell-mell in to it, seasoned with pepper and salt and chile.*

George Ruxton (11)

*The good lady of the house sent me a huge bowl of atole as I was engaged in clothing the animals, which I offered to Panchito as soon as the messenger's back was turned, and he swallowed it, boiling hot as it was, with great gusto.*

George Ruxton (12)

*The staple productions of the country are emphatically Indian corn and wheat. The former grain is most extensively employed for making tortillas – an article of food greatly in demand among the people, the use of which has been transmitted to them by the aborigines. The corn is boiled in water with a little lime; and when it has been sufficiently softened, so as to strip it from its skin, it is ground into paste upon the metate and formed into a thin cake. This is afterwards spread on a thin sheet of iron or copper called comal and placed over the fire, where in less than three minutes it is baked and ready for use. The thinness of the tortilla is always a great test of skill in the maker, and much rivalry ensues in the art of preparation.*

Josiah Gregg (13)

# Foods of the Early American West

*Captain Jose Hernanodez invited me to "cinar" [supper] with him - bread, cheese and such.*

Matthew Field (14)

*Here I was made welcome by the Indian family, who prepared a supper of frijoles and atole, the last the dish of New Mexico. It is made of Indian Meal, mixed with water into a thick gruel, and thus eaten – an insipid compound. Far more agreeable is the pinole of the tierra afuera, which is the meal of parched maize, mixed with sugar and spices and of which a handful in a pint of water makes a most cooling and agreeable drink, and is the standby of the arrieros and road travelers in the starving country.*

George Ruxton (15)

*A sort of thin mush called atole, made of Indian meal, as another sort of diet the preparation of which is from the aborigines; and such is its nationality that in the north it is frequently called "el café de los Mexicanos". How general so ever the use of coffee among the Americans may appear, that of atole is still more so among the lower classes of Mexicans. They virtually breakfast, dine and sup on it. Of this indeed, with frijoles and chile (beans and red pepper), consists their principle food.*

Josiah Gregg (16)

What we see over and over in the food of this region is good, basic foods that provided the nourishment not only for the Hispanics who lived in the area, but for the white travelers who visited and settled there. These southwestern foods were the most written about food besides the buffalo by the White men who visited the west. All of it made an impression on them and their stomachs.

1. Lewis Garrard, *Wah-to-yah and the Taos Trail*, University of Oklahoma Press, Norman, 1957, page 175.
2. Garrard, page 227.
3. James Webb, *Adventures in the Santa Fe Trade*, *Adventures in the Santa Fe Trade 1844-1847*, Ralph Bieber editor, University of Nebraska, Lincoln, 1995, page 104.
4. George Brewerton, *Overland with Kit Carson*, University of Nebraska, Lincoln, 1993, page 177.
5. Matthew Field, *Matt Field on the Santa Fe Trail*, John Sunder editor, University of Oklahoma Press, Norman, 1995, page 195.
6. Field, pages 203-204.
7. Garrard, page 231.
8. Joseph Williams, *Narrative of a Tour from the State of Indiana to the Oregon Territory*

*in the Years 1841-2*, Ye Galleon Press, Fairfield, 1977, page 55.

9.  Thomas James, *Three Years among the Indians and Mexicans*, *Three Years Among the Indians and Mexicans*, Milo Quaife editor, Citadel Press, New York, 1966, page 147.

10. Ruxton, page 197. (The tortilla is a round flat pancake, made of the Indian cornmeal; the gordita is of the same material, but thicker.)

11. Ruxton, *Ruxton of the Rockies*, page 156.

12. Ruxton, *Ruxton of the Rockies*, page 190.

13. Josiah Gregg, *Commerce of the Prairies*, Milo Milton Quaife editor, University of Nebraska Press, Lincoln, 1967, page 146.

14. Field, page 51.

15. Ruxton, *Ruxton of the Rockies*, page 188.

16. Gregg, page 147.

# Native American Influences

*We went in to a lodge… water was handed us to drink, as they suppose a traveler would be thirsty after riding; then meat was set before us, as they think a tired man needs refreshment. When we had finished, the pipe was passed around, during which soothing pastime the news were asked.*

Lewis Garrard (1)

*The bowls held about three quarts each of boiled maize, which had been protractedly simmering over the fire had acquired a consistency between that of porridge and paste. This gluteinous mass was to be swallowed without the aid of milk, salt, water or any other assistant what so ever, and to crown my misfortunes, I had already been to two common feasts, and had taken my usual quantum of dinner before I arrived at this great medicine-invitation.*

Charles Murray (2)

T O get a complete idea of Native American influence in the west and its food, the reader needs to combine what is written so far, to put away all that is previously thought on the topic of this group's food (like that the people only ate buffalo all the time) and associate other not thought of edibles, like vegetables, discussed in a previous chapter. I always say history is complicated and it is. When we think of historic foods, it is not any different. Indian foods like Camas Root, Pemmican and dried meat will be talked about and shown in other chapters of this book, so be sure to investigate these items when adding up this group's influence. Here are a few entries that will start us off in our search for the truth of what the various tribes ate:

*One had a small piece of dried salmon another a few handfuls of corn, some dried roots each bringing something & insisted that we should eat.*

James Clyman (3)

*For food provisions, which come first of all, this is the order followed. First of all, the* plats-cotes *are set aside for immediate use. They are prepared by roasting. Also used immediately are the bony parts of the hump, which are boiled, and the stomach, which is cut into strips and either boiled or roasted. The choice cuts, capable of being preserved, such as the tongue or the top of the hump, are kept for festive occasions. The pieces destined to serve as daily provisions are first cut into slices and either dried or smoked, and then beaten with a wooden mallet, to make them tender or to enable them to be packed away more closely in the packing boxes. Thus stored away, they can be preserved for months or even years and may be eaten either raw or cooked.*

Nicholas Point (4)

The native tribes had generations of experience to help them know what a good food was. They not only used and traded various dried meats; they also had a market for it. All around them in their claimed territories were all that they needed to survive. They used much of what we will see recorded here daily from that gathering area. Since some of their foods and the ways they were prepared are much different than what most Whites knew about, we will see a number of references into the Native tribes' preparations and food sources in the referenced white's writings, since the original viewer found it interesting to mention it in their journals. You should also remember and note that each region and tribe had different main food sources, depending on where they lived, what game/plants were located there and the philosophies/practices the tribes had with their meals and banquets.

*In pursuance of my plan I endeavored by all means in my power to procure a guide but could not succeed. I therefore got the best instruction I could in regard to the route and collected a supply of corn, beans, locust bread and a little Indian flour.*

Jedediah Smith (5)

*The game had to be distributed, but in what proportion? This is the rule: the*

112

*hunter who made the kill had a right to the hide and half the animal, minus the head and legs. The latter belong to the community. The distribution was made in the lodge of the chief, but before proceeding with it, a prayer was said.*

Father Nicholas Point (6)

Jacob Robinson gives us insight to what he saw when staying and eating with the inhabitants of a village he calls "Lagoona":

*They insisted upon our eating with them. Their food consists mostly of melons, pumpkins and parched corn, but they make a singular kind of paste bread, which in appearance very much resembles a hornet's nest and which they prepare with great care and skill, in the following manner: they choose a flat rock, two feet wide by three or four long, and six or eight inches thick; make it quite smooth on top, and kindle a good fire beneath it; when the stone is hot enough for their purpose, fine Indian meal mixed thin with water is poured and spread rapidly over the smooth hot surface, and is thus cooked instantaneously. The bread comes off as smooth as the surface of the rock, is about as thick as common paper, is folded up after the manner of a newspaper, and being quite flexible, and the corn from which it is made being blue, its color is exactly that of a hornet's nest. This bread, when packed up, is excellent for a journey. (7)*

There are many foods we see associated with these first people, much written about in the many chapters here, but there are two special foods which are connected to these groups that need to be written about here: dog and camas root.

I cannot write about this ethnic group's contribution to foods, without noting Lewis Garrard's encounter with dog meat and how he first said he would never eat it, but liked it when it was served to him unknowingly. And the great story of John Smith teasing him about eating dog in the village and liking it.

*I bet I'll make you eat dog meat in the village and you'll say it is good, and the best you ever hid in your meat-bag (stomach). "No, you will not" he replied, "the mere idea is enough to sicken me – slimy pup meat! Ugh!*

*[later] I asked him what was on the fire. Terripins! Promptly replied Smith. Terripins? I echoed, in surprise at the name. Terripins! How do you cook them? You know them hard shelled land Terripins? Yes. Well, the [women] go out to the sand buttes, and bring the critters in, and cook'em in the shell alive- those stewin' thar are cleaned first. Howsoever, they're darmed good!*

*Yes, hos, an' that's a fact, wagh! Chimed in Greenwood.*

*I listened, of course, with much interest to their account of the savage dish,*

**113**

*and waited, with impatience for a taste of that… I ate it with much gusto, calling "for more". It was extremely good, and I spoke of the delicacy of the meat and answered all their questions as to its excellency in the affirmative, even to the extent of a panegyric on the whole turtle species. After fully committing myself, Smith looked at me awhile in silence, the corners of his mouth gradually making preparations for a laugh, and asked: "Well, hos, how do you like dog meat?" … A revulsion of opinion, and dog meat too, ensued, for I could feel the "pup" crawling up my throat; but saying to myself – {that it was good under the name of terrapin, and that a rose under any other name would be just as sweet" and that it would be prejudice to stop…ever after remained a stanch defender and admirer or dog meat… and I acknowledged that "dog" was next in order to buffalo."*

Lewis Garrard (8)

Many early travelers had the same preconceived notions on this animal, but it seems all who tasted it; liked it.

*Old Smoke had a fat puppy killed and put in to the kettle for us this morning. It was excellent.*

Francis Parkman (9)

*We passed to-day several large lodges of Indians, from whom we wished to have purchased fish, but they had none, or were not willing to spare any, so that we were compelled to purchase a dog for supper. I have said we, but I beg leave to correct myself, as I was utterly averse to the proceeding; not, however, from any dislike to the quality of the food, (I have eaten it repeatedly, and relished it) but am always unwilling, unless when suffering absolute want, to take the life of so noble and faithful an animal. Our hungry oarsmen, however, appeared to have no such scruples. The Indian called his dog, and he came to him, wagging his tail! He sold his companion for ten balls and powder! One of our men approached the poor animal with an axe. I turned away my hear to avoid the sight, but I heard the dull, sodden sound of the blow. The tried friend and faithful companion lay quivering in the agonies of death at its master's feet.*

John Townsend (10)

Another food staple for some of the tribes was a root called Camas. You will see it spelled a number of ways in the journals, dairies and autobiographies, but all the spellings mean the same plant.

*Mean time I had got some dried meat for supper, and the dried fruit of a sort of service tree* [service berries], *and a handful of biscuit root to eat…*

William Drummond Stewart (11)

`Kamas in bloom, the Indians are taking large quantities of it.*
Nathaniel Wyeth (12)

*The Bitter Root [River] is so named after a bitter root which the Indians eat. They make a feast on it, which is agreeable to the taste. It is a white root with three or four prongs; very pleasant to the palate after one has become accustomed to eating it. It fills the place of bread fruit and would be a good substitute. Another root called commace, is baked like a "pone" of bread and they slice it off.*
Robert Campbell (13)

*The camas grows here in abundance, and it is the principal resort of the Cayuses and many other tribes, to obtain it, as they are very fond of it. It resembles an onion in shape and color, when cooked is very sweet and tastes like a fig. Their manner of cooking them is very curious: They dig a hole in the ground, throw in a heap of stones, heat them to a red heat, cover them with green grass, upon which they put the camas, and cover the whole with earth. When taken out it is black. This is the chief food of many tribes during winter.*
Narcissa Whitman (14)

Whitman's drawing of a Camas root.

*During our journey, I witnessed the process of cooking "Kamas," a small root about the size of a crab apple, which abounds in many parts of this country, in the rich bottoms that border most of the streams and rivers. The mode of preparing this root, is almost identical with that by which the south sea Islanders cook their cannibal and swinish food, and the west Indians their plantain. The squaws, by whom all the avocations of domestic labor are performed, excavate round holes in the earth two feet deep, and three in diameter, which are then filled with dry wood and stones in alternate layers, and the fuel fired beneath. When the wood consumes the heated stones fall to the bottom, and are then covered with a layer of grass, upon which two or three bushels of kamas roots, according to the capacity of the whole, are placed, and covered with a layer of grass, and the whole coated over with earth, upon which a large fire is kept burning for fifteen hours. Time is then allowed for the kamas to cool, when the hole is opened, and if perfectly done, the roots which were before white, are now of a deep black color, not disagreeable to the taste, and having something the flavor of liquorice. Thus prepared, the kamas is both edible and nutritious, and forms no inconsiderable item of food with many of the Rocky Mountain tribes.*

Warren Ferris (15)

An endnote by the editor of *Edward Warren*, says camas is also called biscuit root here, better known as kammas:

*Which is of a sweet and glutinous nature, tasting exactly like a New York cracker newly baked.* (16)

*...we chewed some pieces of kamas, which resemble jujube [a plum like fruit of certain old World trees of the zizyphus] and 431 (note) says it resembles a tulip bulb and is a gummy substance, sweet tasting.*

William Drumond Stewart (17)

Rufus Sage (18) mentions two kinds of roots and how they were prepared. Not all of the foods we see connected with Whites/Indians were strange to the later:

*...Indian feast that included an animal they had never ate before. When he drew a picture of it in the sand, they did not believe an animal like that ever existed, since they had seen all the animals.*

Jacob Fowler (18)

You see a lot on western Native American foods in this book. Its influence on the western scene cannot be overlooked. Please remember to connect what was written here to other food sources found elsewhere in the book to give you a good overall idea on this.

1. Lewis Garrard, *Wah-to-yah and the Taos Trail*, University of Oklahoma Press, Norman, 1957, page 49.
2. Charles Murray, *Travels in North America*, William Blackwood and Sons, Edinburgh, 1900, pages 208-9.
3. James Clyman, *Journal of a Mountain* Man, Mountain Press Publishing, Missoula, 1984, page 126.
4. Nicholas Point, *Wilderness Kingdom*, Loyola Press, Chicago, 1967, pages 128-9.
5. Jedediah Smith, *A Southwest Expedition of Jedediah Smith*, University of Nebraska Press, Lincoln, 1989, page 78.
6. Point, page 180.
7. Garrard, pages 47-9.
8. Francis Parkman, *The Journals of Francis Parkman*, Harper and Brothers, New York, 1947 (two volumes), page 443.
9. John Townsend, page 246.
10. Sir William Drummond Steward, *Edward Warren*, page 161. [The endnote in this book labels this biscuit root lomatium cous.]
11. Nathaniel Wyeth, *Across the Rockies to the Columbia*, University of Nebraska Press, 1978, page 54.
12. Robert Campbell, *A Narrative of Colonel Robert Campbell's, Experiences in the Rocky Mountain Fur Trade from 1825-1835*, Drew Hollway, editor, Ye Galleon Press, Fairfield, Washington, 1999, page 28.
13. Narcissa Whitman, *My Journal*, University of Nebraska Press, Lincoln, 1989, page 34.
14. Warren Ferris, *Life in the Rocky Mountains*, Old West Publishing, Denver, 1983, pages 173-4.
15. Stewart, page 161. [He also offers other comments on plant, pages 206 208 431n.]
16. Steward, *Edward Warren*, page 208.
17. Rufus Sage, *Rocky Mountain Life*, University of Nebraska Press, Lincoln, 1982, page 147.
18. Jacob Fowler, *The Journal of Jacob Fowler*, Elliot Coues editor, Ross & Haines, Inc., Minneapolis, 1965, page 73.

# Foods of Necessity

*(or "Ten-o-sast?" — Cheyenne for what is it?)*

"Old horse, old horse,
*what brought you here!*
*From Saracen's head to Portland pier,*
*I've carted stone many a year;*
*Till killed by blows and sore abuse,*
*They've salted me down for sailor's use."*

George Brewerton (1)

**F**OR me to add to what the journals tell us about their foods when they were without resources to replenish their food supplies while in tight spots would be blasphemy. So here in their own words are the many different foods they ate when they did not have a choice:

*This was the first occasion subjecting me to the pains of hunger for so long a time. The second day I experienced the greatest annoyance, and then it was I felt some of the realities of starvation. The third day, however, I awoke in the morning scarcely thinking of breakfast. In fact, my appetite seemed quite passive, and the only sensation I felt was a kind of weakness and lassitude, evincing the last of proper nourishment.*

Rufus Sage (2)

119

John Townsend relates another story told to him by his traveling companion, Richardson on how he survived after being robbed by a tribe and left with nothing, Richardson says in his own words *"Why, set to trappin' prairie squirrel with little nooses made out of the hairs of my head."* (3)

James Pattie thought horse flesh to be as bad as he feared it would be:

*Desirous of returning to some settlement, my father encouraged our party to eat some of the horses, and pursue our journey. We were all reluctant to begin to partake of horse-flesh; and the actual thing without bread or salt was as bad as the anticipations of it... (4)*

Many had experienced this meat at least once in this life.

*... he gave us a horse to eat of which he had 260 in fine order and of good breed we found the meat equal to any beef and quite different from the poor and sick old ones we had eaten.*

Nathaniel Wyeth (5)

*Here is my off-wheel mule, Poor old Ned, said Enoch Barnes, one of the Americans in our party. We killed the mule and took off all his meat, packing it on the rear of our saddles... there we feasted on sweet mule-meat, without salt.*

James Hobbs (6)

*I observed a beautiful, sleek colt, of about four months old, trot into camp, whinnying with great apparent pleasure and dancing and curveting gaily amongst our sober and sedate band. I had no doubt he had strayed from Indians...but as here, every animal that comes near us was fair game, as we were hungry, not having eaten anything of consequence since yesterday morning, I thought the little stranger would make a good breakfast for us. Concluding, however, that it would be best to act advisedly in the matter, I put my head into captain W's tent, and telling him news, made the proposition which had occurred to me. The captain's reply was encouraging enough – "Down with him, if you please, Mr. T., it is the Lord's doing; let us have him for breakfast."*

John Townsend (7)

*The fourth day, our bacon and bread gave out and we had nothing to eat. The fifth day, the largest game we saw was jack-ass rabbits, of which we killed two and divided among the company of eighteen persons. On the sixth day, I shot a wolf, but its flesh was so poor and bad flavored, that we could not eat it...*

James Hobbs (8)

A great entry on horse meat was written by George Brewerton:

*But then the contemplation of horse-meat, as an edible, had been with me but an abstract idea, which I had never contemplated, putting into practice. Now, however, the thing was tangible. To eat or not to eat, became "the question", and after due consideration, hunger arguing the case on one side, with strong necessity for an advocate – and fastidiousness taking the opposite, with prejudice for her backer, I came to the conclusion that I would not and could not eat horse-flesh. In accordance with this valorous decision, although upon our arrival at camp, a horse (lean, old and decidedly tough) was actually killed, cut up and freely eaten of, I alone stood aloof, and went to bed supperless. But it was all in vain; for starvation is a weighty reason, and hunger gained the day at last. I stood out like a Trojan for eighty four hours, and then "gave in" with as good a grace as possible and for more than a week ate horseflesh regularly. Perhaps the reader would like to know how it tasted. I can only say that it was an old animal, a tough animal, and a sore backed animal – and upon the whole – I prefer beef.*

*Indeed, we had already eaten the next thing to mule and nothing – broken down steer meat. Oh grief! My jaws ache to think of the sobby "dejeners", in the soaking rain, of old steer, or, as the Canadians termed it "sacre beef". (9)*

Horses and steers were not the only foods used when in a pinch:

*Upon the opposite side of the river was a bald-eagle's nest, with two half-grown fledglings. One of our party, ascending the tree, captured the young ones, and we had a fine meal from their carcasses.*

Rufus Sage (10)

*Last night in cutting a tree for fuel caught two young grey eagles one of which we ate and found it tender and good.*

Nathaniel Wyeth (11)

*We have in this country a large kind of black cricket 2 inches long said to be used as food by the Indians, they are in great numbers and roost on the sage at noon day.*

Nathaniel Wyeth (12)

The book *Covered Wagon Women* has two good entries on what they resorted to in the wagon trains when times got tough. In the first one, they shot one of their work oxen. And on the same page, two captured whites where robbed by the Pawnees and lived on berries and rose-buds till they arrived at civilization. (13)

*In fact, we should have long before have been in danger of starvation had it not been for our oxen; for we had seen a buffalo since the first day... Some of our cattle being in good plight and able as we were to spare a few from our teams, we made beef of them when urged by necessity; an extra advantage in ox teams on these perilous expeditions.*

Josiah Gregg (14)

Other forms of survival food did not show up on four legs. There were many different plants that the men sought nourishment in.

*...several of the men sought a temporary respite from the torments of hunger by eating roasted cacti- the article at first tasted well, and from the recommendations of the essayists, several were induced to partake of it quite heartily.*

*But the lapse of a brief hour or two bought with it the "tug of war" when the inherent properties of the cacti began to have their effect upon the enervated systems of the participants.*

*The painful consequences of this strange diet at first were a weakness in the joints, succeeded by a severe trembling and a desire to vomit, accompanied with an almost insufferable pain in the stomach and bowels. Three or four of the unfortunate sufferers were in such extreme pain they rolled on the ground in agony, with countenances writhing in every imaginable shape of frightful distortion. Hereupon it was decided to sacrifice one of our animals as a last resort, which was promptly done, and we ended our fast of nearly seven days' continuance with a feast of mule meat. I had heretofore cherished a decided repugnance to this kind of food, but an in justice bound to say, it proved both sweet and tender and scarcely inferior to beef.* (15)

One meat that was considered to be a survival food that caused many who ate it problems afterwards was beaver. This problem only seemed to be a regional ailment.

*...those who eat their meat in a few hours become sick at the stomach and the whole system is filled with cramps and severe pains, but I have never known or heard of a person's dying with this disease.*

Osborne Russell (16)

*The river on which we were now encamped, and the fortunate and timely discovery of which had saved us from the last extremity of thirst, is called 'La Riviere Maladi,' (Sick River,) and owes its name to the fact that the beaver found upon it, if eaten by the unwary hunter, causes him to have a singular fit, the symptoms of which are, stiffness of the neck, pains in the bones, and nervous contortions of the face. A party of half-starved trappers found their way to this stream a few years since, and observing plenty of beaver 'signs,' immediately set their traps, in order to procure provisions. At dawn the next day, several fine large fat beavers were taken, and skinned, dressed and cooked, with the least possible delay. The hungry trappers fed ravenously upon the smoking viands, and soon left scarce a single bone unpicked. Two or three hours elapsed, when several of the party were seized with a violent cramp in the muscles of the neck; severe shooting pains darted through the frame, and the features became hideously convulsed. Their companions were greatly alarmed at their condition, and imagined them to be in imminent danger. However, at the expiration of an hour, they were quite recovered, but others had meantime been attacked in the same way... I do not believe a single one of us will ever be induced to try the same experiment again, no matter how urgently pressed by starvation.*

Warren Ferris (17)

Robert Campbell's journal is another which recorded those who ate beaver and had pains afterward.

*One of my men caught a beaver. We had nothing to eat. My French cook roasted the beaver. I ate a small piece to quiet my appetite, as I had had nothing to eat for a day or two. Just after I ate, I felt pains, as did all the others who ate it. The beavers were poisoned from eating the wild parsnip. Hence the name of the river, Malade. Everyone who ate these beavers were poisoned...we had pains in the neck, head and other disagreeable sensations in the stomach and bowels. The old trappers knew what was the matter and attributed our sickness to eating of poisoned beaver.* (18)

*...in the morning, our hunter went out and wounded a deer which the wolves ran down, but before he could find him, they had eaten up all but enough for 2 meals...*

Nathaniel Wyeth (19)

123

It does not require a very experienced baker to show that, if attempted to furnish bread to four men out of this stock, even allowing six ounces to each per diem, it would very soon be exhausted, and I suggested an expedient which succeeded beyond our most sanguine expectations. It was simply this, to give up altogether our fried flour cakes, and to make our morning and evening meal consist of a pot of buffalo broth, into which we could still afford to throw a few beans and grains of maize. When the whole was well boiled and ready for the table, while it was simmering over the fire, we took half a pint of flour and dropped it slowly into the soup, stirring the later with a spoon of stick; in this manner it soon became soft and thick as gruel, and we found it a most palatable and nutritious food. Thus used, a pint of flour among four men is sufficient allowance, and will satisfy hunger as much as two or three quarts made into bread or cakes. We discovered another excellent quality of this soup – that it allayed, or rather prevented the cravings of thirst for a longer period than any other food…

Charles Murray (20)

In warm weather there is a fly, about the size and similar to a grain of wheat, on this lake, in great numbers. – When the wind rolls the waters onto the shore, these flies are left on the beach – the female Indians then carefully gather them into baskets made of willow branches and lay them exposed to the sun until they become perfectly dry, when they are laid away for winter provender. These flies, together with grass seed, and a few rabbits is their principle food during the winter season.

Zenas Leonard (21)

Other forms of survival foods:

… they said they had not known whether we were before or in the rear, that they had eaten nothing for the last two days, and that night they had intended to have boiled a deer skin to subsist on.

Zebulon Pike (22)

On the 24th, the hunter killed three fat buffalo, which was the first fat meal we had seen for twenty days. We all ate a large quantity of the raw tallow.

E. Willard Smith (23)

Having nothing prepared for dinner to-day, I strolled along the stream above the camp, and made a meal on rose buds, of which I collected abundance; and on returning, I was surprised to find Mr. N. and Captain T. picking the last bones of a bird which they had cooked. Upon inquiry, I ascertained that the subject was an unfortunate owl which I had killed in the morning, and had intended to preserve, as a specimen…

John Townsend (24)

[after four days of separation from his group and only one meal since then] *As I was winding my way through the trees, I heard a loud click above me, and observed a large red squirrel spring in from one limb to another of a bur oak... I was hungry, and this cowardly maneuver made me angry, I determined, that have that squirrel I would, if I spent the whole day shooting at him. I rested the rifle against the trunk of a tree, and after a long aim, fired; the bullet dashed the head of the little animal to pieces, and whirled him some twenty feet in the air.*

*I had lost my knife on the day previous, but with the assistance of a nail I found in my pouch, I skinned my prize, and impaling him upon the point of a spit I made of a dry stick, stuck it in the ground before the fire to roast.*

John Treat Irving (25)

*The stream itself was generally three quarters of a mile in width, with a current of five miles per hour, water three and half foot deep and of a chalky whiteness. It was extremely sweet – so delicious that some of my men declared it an excellent substitute for milk. ... Here I shall be expected by those civilized monsters who live by eating and drinking, to give a description of the manner of making this soup. It was indeed a rare dish. And my friends of the trencher – ye who have been spiced and peppered and salted from your youth up, do not distort your nasal protuberances when I declare that of all the vulgar innovations upon kitchen science that civilization has parched upon the good old style of the patriarchs, nothing has produced so beastly effect upon taste, as the self same condiments of salt, pepper & c. Woeful heresy! Human nature peppered and salted! An abomination in my humble opinion, that calls for the full force of this world's moral and physical posse to exterminate. But to our soup. It was made of simple meat and water of pure water, such as kings drank...*

Thomas Farnham (26)

Let's hope we never get in a condition that we have to use a few of these historically correct and kind of odd foods to survive on. But if you ever do, you now know that you were not the first to find this solution.

1. George Brewerton, *Overland with Kit Carson*, University of Nebraska, Lincoln, 1993, page 124.
2. Rufus Sage, *Rocky Mountain Life*, University of Nebraska Press, Lincoln, 1982, page 136.
3. John Kirk Townsend, *Across the Rockies to the Columbia*, University of Nebraska Press, Lincoln, 1978, page 140.
4. James Pattie, *The Personal Narrative of James O. Pattie*, University of Nebraska Press, Lincoln, 1984, page 50.
5. Nathaniel J. Wyeth, *The Journals of Captain Nathaniel J. Wyeth's Expeditions to the*

*Oregon Country, 1831-1836,* Ye Galleon Press, Fairfield, 1997, page 28.

6. James Hobbs, *Wild Life in the Far West,* Rio Grande Press, Glorieta, 1969, page 69.
7. Townsend, pages 43-44.
8. Hobbs, page 68.
9. Brewerton, page 124.
10. Sage, page 187.
11. Wyeth, page 11.
12. Wyeth, page 19.
13. Kenneth Holmes, *Covered Wagon Women* (volume one), University of Nebraska Press, Lincoln, 1983, page 57.
14. Josiah Gregg, *Commerce of the Prairies,* Milo Milton Quaife editor, University of Nebraska Press, Lincoln, 1967, page 226.
15. Sage, page 307.
16. Osborne Russell, *Journal of a Trapper,* University of Nebraska Press, Lincoln, 1986, page 124.
17. Warren Ferris, *Life in the Rocky Mountains,* Old West Publishing, Denver, 1983, pages 139-140.
18. Robert Campbell, *A Narrative of Colonel Robert Campbell's, Experiences in the Rocky Mountain Fur Trade from 1825-1835,* Drew Hollway, editor, Ye Galleon Press, Fairfield, Washington, 1999, pages 28-9.
19. Wyeth, page 94.
20. Charles Murray, *Travels in North America,* William Blackwood and Sons, Edinburgh, 1900, pages 303-4.
21. Zenas Leonard, *Adventures of a Mountain Man,* Milo Quaife editor, University of Nebraska Press, Lincoln, 1978, pages 118-9.
22. Zebulon Pike,*The Southwest Journals of Zebulon Pike,* Stephen Hart & Archer Hulbert editors, University of New Mexico Press, Albuquerque, 2006, page 161.
23. E. Willard Smith, Colorado Magazine, *With the Fur Traders of Colorado,* July 1950, page 180.
24. Townsend, page 167.
25. John Treat Irving, *Indian Sketches,* University of Oklahoma Press, Norman, 1955, pages 230-1.
26. Thomas Farnham, private reprint by Don Erickson and Bob Elsloo, 2007, pages 27-8.

# Cooking Methods

*The roll has been called, and each mess is preparing breakfast. I hear Dr. Trask courteously ask: "Are those plates clean?" and Rhoades's nonchalant answer: "To be sure they are, didn't we eat off them last night?"*

John Audubon (1)

**U**P to now, we have discussed the many different foods found in the early American west. But how did they cook or process all these foods? Let's see what the journal writings have to teach us on this subject. Just as we read in our opening quote for this chapter, health standards were a lot different than today.

> *We are tired of life in this dirty fort to the highest degree. Our daily routine is conducted in such a filthy manner that it nauseated one. Since our Negro cook Alfred suffers a severe rheumatic disease, we now have a filthy attendant and cook named Boileau who wears a fur cap, sits down among us and handles the cups and plates with his disgusting fists, after cleaning his nose according to the manner of our peasants.*
>
> Prince Maximilian (2)

Meals were not prepared over modern-style forms of heat. All the western individuals used what was available to them or what they brought with them (which was not much). All cooking, if any form of cooking was done, had a fire involved with the process. No electricity, no microwaves, nonstick pans, blenders and no modern ovens were to be found in their permanent or moveable camps. Nathaniel Wyeth will start this section off with what he saw at a meal:

> *...our fires look finely with sundry roasting sticks around full of meat...* (3)

Preparation of food then was just an everyday event and many made it look easy. Even the huge buffalo which was a virtual Seven-Eleven on legs was not a monumental work. Nicholas Point wrote:

> *...after it was skinned, the tongue, legs, and all parts that may serve some purpose was removed. For a good hunter, this is a matter of twenty –thirty minutes work.* (4)

Having helped with five or six skinnings and butcherings of these big animals, I can safely say getting the hide off is a chore in itself, the quartering, separating internal organs, keeping everything clean and getting them ready for a move to camp takes time. Thomas Farnum shows us how he butchered such an animal where it was shot:

> *...We butchered him in the following manner: having turned him upon his brisket, and split the skin along the spine; and pared off the hide as far down the sides as his position would allow, we cut off the flesh that lay outside the ribs as far back as the loins. This the hunters call "the fleece." We next took the ribs that rise perpendicularly from the spine between the shoulders and support what is termed "the hump." The we laid our heavy wood axes upon the enormous side ribs, opened the cavity, and took out the tender loins, tallow, c... all this a load for two mules to*

*carry into camp.* (5)

It seems everyone had a different way to prepare the animal for use and remove the meat. Phillip Covington gives a good description of cooking the buffalo (just barely done!) in a pot. (6)

*The process of butchering was a new development of that most useful science. The carcass was first turned upon the belly, and braced to a position by its distended legs. The operator then commenced his labors by gathering the long hair of the "boss," and severing a piece obliquely at the junction of the neck and shoulders, —then parting the hide from neck to rump, a few passes of his ready knife laid bare the sides, —next paring away the loose skin and preparing a hold, with one hand he pulled the shoulder towards him and with the other severed it from the body;— cutting aslant the uprights of the spina dorsi and "hump ribs," along the lateral to the curve, and parting the "fleece" from the tough flesh at that point he deposited it upon a clean grass-spot. The same process being described upon the opposite side, the carcass was then slightly inclined, and, by aid of the leg-bone bisected at the knee joint, the "hump-ribs" were parted from the vertebra; after which, passing his knife aside the ninth rib and around the ends at the midriff, he laid hold of the dissevered side, and, with two or three well directed jerks, removed it to be laid upon his choicely assorted pile; a few other brief minutia then completed the task.*

Rufus Sage (7)

Hasting's *Emigrant Guide* gives the western traveler some advice when it came to their kitchen for their western food preparation:

*Very few cooking utensils should be taken, as they very much increase the load, to avoid which, is always a consideration of paramount importance. A baking-kettle, frying pan, tea kettle, tea pot, and coffee pot, are all furniture of this kind, that is essential, which together with tin plates, tin cups, ordinary knives, forks, spoons and a coffee mill, should constitute the entire kitchen apparatus.* (8)

The famous author, Washington Irving, described in his journal how they set the "table" at one of his parties' camp:

*Blankets had been spread on the ground near to the fire, upon which we took our seats. A large dish, or bowl, made from the root of a maple tree, and which we had purchased at the Indian village, was placed on the ground before us, and into it were emptied the contents of one of the camp-kettles, consisting of a wild turkey hashed, together with slices of bacon and lumps of dough. Beside it was placed another bowl of similar ware, containing an ample supply of fritters. After we had discussed the hash,*

**129**

*two wooden splits, on which the ribs of a fat buck were broiling before the fire, were removed and planted in the ground before us, with a triumphant air, by little Tonish. Having no dishes, we had to proceed in hunter's style, cutting off strips and slices with our hunting knives, and dipping them in to the salt and pepper... With all this, our beverage was coffee, boiled in a camp-kettle, sweetened with brown sugar, and drunk of our tin cups...* (9)

*Some meat, probably brought in from the surround, was hung over a tripod, it was a magnificent depouile, lined with three fingers of fat at least.*

Sir William Drummond Stewart (10)

Alfred Jacob Miller, describing his painting "Breakfast at Sunrise" explained on the back of the artwork what he saw there when making the pen and watercolor:

*This sketch represents "our mess" at the morning meal, Francois pouring out the coffee. The dishes on the table, or rather on the India-rubber cloth, were of block-tin, and the etiquette was quite rigid in some particulars; for instance, nothing like a fork, or substitute was used, without you wished to raise a storm of ridicule about your ears. With the "bowie knife" you separated a rib from the mass in the center of the table, seizing with your hand the lower end and cutting away a la discretion. We had no bread the entire journey. The attitude at meals was generally cross legged, a la mode Oriental. Indians were meanwhile patiently standing near, in order to be ready for the 'second table' eating enough at once to suffice them for three days.*

*On one occasion, our Commander, who had purchased some boxes of sardine at St. Louis (intending to keep them in reserve for sickness or other emergency) ordered one of them to be placed on the 'table.' It was a double box, and contained about a pint. A trapper opened it, pronounced the contents fish, and emptied the whole on his plate. Seeing this, the Captain ordered out the whole lot of sardines, as he saw that nothing short of it would go round. He would not for the world have hinted to them that it was customary to eat only two to three as a relish. This breakfast must have cost him upwards of sixty dollars, but it furnished him a capital after-dinner story for Europe, and he considered that worth all the money.* (11)

One other point which should be made about cooking and traveling through this region: wood for cook fires was hard to come by, except near the streams. So, in most areas on the plains the scarcity of wood prompted the use of sun-dried buffalo dung as fuel. Charles Murray writes:

*Of this strange fuel they brought in great quantity; when once thoroughly ignited it burns well, emits a strong heat, and its smell is not so offensive as might be expected.* (12)

But Murray did not do as the others around him who threw their meat directly on the fire to cook. He kept his out of the buffalo-chip fire when grilling his buffalo.

*Dried buffalo dung, which we now find quite frequently, we now use occasionally for fuel, when absolutely no wood can be found. It burns tolerably well, but makes rather a glow than a flaming fire, adequate for cooking, but small comfort in severe cold.* (13)

*The lack of wood at this place was readily met by the great abundance of bois de vache (buffalo chips) the common substitute of the prairies; and in a brief interval, the camp-fires were merrily blazing, with all the appliances of cooking around them.*
Rufus Sage (14)

Times may change, but cooking was done in a lot of ways, no different than in our modern kitchens. One does all the cooking and many stand around and wait for it to be done.

*Our Camp Kettle had not been greased for some time: as we were continually boiling thistle roots in them during the day: but now four of them containing about three gallons each were soon filled with fat bear meat cut in very small pieces and hung over a fire which all hands were employed in keeping up with the utmost impatience. An old experienced hand who stood about six feet six and never in a hurry about anything was selected by a unanimous vote to say when the stew (as we called it) was done but I thought with my comrades that it took a longer time to cook than any meal ever saw prepared, and after repeated appeals to his lone and hungry stewardship by all hands present he consented that it might be seasoned with salt and pepper and dish it out to cool. But it had not much time for cooling before we commended operations:*

*all pronounced it the best meal they ever had.*

Osborne Russell (15)

*...When that incomparable piece, the hump rib, is brought into camp, Jean, our Chef, at once takes charge of it, and the manner in which he prepares it for the table, although simple enough, is perfection. He skewers it lengthwise, with a stick sharpened at one end, leaving sufficient room at the other to plant it in the ground near the fire, inclining inward at the top. When done, it exceeds in flavor, richness and juiciness, any beef we have ever tasted, and this judgment will be confirmed by all who have ever partaken of the glorious 'hump rib'.*

Alfred J. Miller (16)

As you can see, the camp kitchens of all races and groups were simple in size and content. And with these few tools they could turn out great food on a regular basis. The following entries emphasize this:

*...I provided myself with a tin plate, a tin cup, which might hold about a quart, for no true mountaineer ever drinks less than that amount of coffee at a sitting-if he can get it. To these articles I added a common fork, a large Bowie knife, and a rifle...*

George Brewerton (17)

*Being already provided with arms, saddles laryettes or tethers, blankets, a bear skin, pack saddles and horses (which last averages about forty dollars apiece) a box of vermilion, to make presents to Indians withal, and a very small assortment of hunting clothes, I provided at the outfitting store the following items: 10 lbs of lead, 6 lbs of shot, 20 lbs of coffee, 12 lbs of salt, an assortment of rings; beads of all colors and sizes; wampum; mirrors, knives, and other trifles for presents. 24 lbs of sugar, three pack blankets and sacks, a bottle of pepper, some tin cups, a bucket, one copper kettle, two tin pans, a frying pan, a jug, two canteens for water, two jugs for brandy, 10 lbs of powder, 50 of bacon for frying, eating, & c... the most important article is not yet included- namely bread or flour, in some shape or other, which is necessary to the extent of 70 or 80 lb for three persons.*

Charles Murray (18)

*Our kitchen utensils consisted of a large iron pot, a smaller tin one for boiling our tea, coffee and & c, and a frying pan without a handle. Our dinner and tea service was not upon so magnificent a scale, having each of us a butcher knife, a tin cup, a wooden bowl and a spoon made of buffalo horn.*

Charles Murray (19)

*...and also my canvas and easel, and our culinary articles which are few and simple; consisting of three tin cups, a coffee pot- one plate- a frying pan- and a tin kettle.*

George Catlin (20)

*My cloak, together with a sack containing some changes of linen and a zinc drinking cup, all fastened to the back of the saddle, made up my total equipment.*

Rudolph Kurz (21)

*A description of the formation of our camp may, perhaps, not be amiss here. The party is divided into messes of eight men, and each mess is allowed a separate tent. The captain of a mess, (who is generally an "old hand," i.e. an experienced forester, hunter, or trapper,) receives each morning the rations of pork, flour, &c. for his people, and they choose one of their body as cook for the whole.*

John Townsend (22)

*The cooking was conducted in hunter's style; the meat was stuck upon tapering spits of dogwood, which were thrust perpendicularly into the ground, so as to sustain the joint before the fire, where it was roasted or broiled with all its juices retained in the manner that would have tickled the palate of the most experienced gourmand...*

Washington Irving (23)

And, after all this information you might think that it was the final

**133**

word on western cooking – but an unusual method was seen in Bryant's journal – he cooked a slab of bacon in a hot spring and it was well cooked in about 15 minutes! (24)

These journal entries give a good idea what they used and carried with them for the preparation of their meals, along with how the larger animals were prepared to transport the meat. Their ways were much different than ours today, but very practical.

1.  John Woodhouse Audubon, *Audubon's Western Journal*, University of Arizona Press, Tucson, 1984, page 119.
2.  Prince Maximilian, *People of the First Man*, Davis Thomas & Karin Ronnefeldt editors, Promontory Press, New York, 1982, pages 200-1.
3.  Nathaniel Wyeth, *The Journals of Captain Nathaniel J. Wyeth's Expeditions to the Oregon Country, 1831-1836*, Ye Galleon Press, Fairfield, 1997, page 91.
4.  Nicholas Point, *Wilderness Kingdom*, Loyola Press, Chicago, 1967, page 125.
5.  Thomas Farnum, private reprint by Don Erickson and Bob Elsoo, 2007, page 30.
6.  Phillip Covington, *Colorado Magazine,* Colorado Historical Society, July, 1950, page 23.
7.  Rufus Sage, *Rocky Mountain Life*, University of Nebraska Press, Lincoln, 1982, page 66.
8.  Lansford Hastings, *The Emigrant's Guide*, Applewood books, Bedford, no date, page 144.
9.  Washington Irving, *A Tour of the Prairies,* University of Oklahoma Press, Norman, 1971, page 58.
10. William Drummond Stewart, *Edward Warren*, Mountain Press, Missoula, 1986,

pages 185 & 187.

11. Michael Bell, *Braves and Buffalo,* University of Toronto Press, Canada, 1973, page 108.

12. Charles Murray, *Travels in North America,* William Blackwood and Sons, Edinburgh, 1900, page 204.

13. Dr. Fredrick Wislizenus, *A Journey to the Rocky Mountains in the Year 1839,* Ye Galleon Press, Fairfield, 1989, pages 43-4.

14. Sage, page 71.

15. Osborne Russell, *Journal of a Trapper,* University of Nebraska Press, Lincoln, 1986, pages 9-10.

16. Bell, page 84.

17. George Brewerton, *Overland with Kit Carson,* University of Nebraska, Lincoln, 1993, pages 39-40.

18. Murray, page 140.

19. Murray, page 279.

20. George Catlin, *Letters and Notes on the North American* Indians, JG Press, North Dighton, 1995, page 76.

21. Rudolph Kurz, *On the Upper Missouri,* Carla Kelly editor, University of Oklahoma Press, Norman, 2005, page 46.

22. John Townsend, *Across the Rockies to the Columbia,* University of Nebraska Press, Lincoln, 1978, page 33.

23. Irving, pages 56-7.

24. Edwin Bryant, *Rocky Mountain Adventures,* Ye Galleon Press, Fairfield, 2000, page 204.

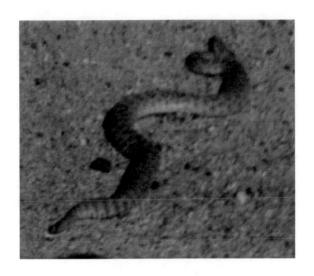

# *Unusual*
# *not*
# *Everyday Cuisine*

*This species of animals* [the porcupines] *are too well known to need a minute description in this place they are however very numerous and their flesh is much esteemed by some of the Indian tribes for food.*

Osborn Russell (1)

**T**HERE is a group of foods that really don't fit anywhere else. They can't be considered staples, are unique to themselves and while historically correct don't show up too often. I will lump these foods into one chapter. I call all this "cuisine," but it will be up to you to decide if any would be found in your menu list. The flesh of the porcupine, which Osborne Russell wrote about to start this chapter, is just one example of the very wide and diverse group which can be called food. Some of what will be written here may sound out of place or a little strange. But, if some creature ate vegetables and bark of trees it was probably considered "food." George Ruxton described the diet of the western individual:

*"Meat's meat" is a common saying in the mountains, and from the buffalo down to the rattlesnake, including every quadruped that runs, every fowl that flies,*

*and every reptile that creeps, nothing comes amiss to the mountaineer. Throwing aside all the qualms and conscientious scruples of a fastidious stomach, it must be confessed that dog-meat takes a high rank in the wonderful variety of cuisine afforded to the gourmand and the gourmet by the prolific mountains. Now when the bill of fare offers such tempting viands as buffalo beef, venisons, mountain mutton, turkey, grouse, wildfowl, hares, rabbits, beaver and their tails & c. & c., the station assigned to "dog" as No. 2 in the list can be well appreciated – No. 1 in delicacy of flavor, richness of meat, and other good qualities, being the flesh of panthers, which surpasses every other, and all put together.* (2)

I would agree with Mr. Ruxton and think of these victuals different than survival foods, not in what they are, but the lengths people go to in having to eat them. Here is an eclectic assortment of unusual main courses (I don't know what else I can call them) found in the old books:

*Here our hunters killed a pelican, as white as snow, and its legs and feet like those of a goose. Its bill is about eighteen inches long, and it has a pouch under its jaw that will hold about three pints. The pelican is about six feet long, its tail short, the flesh coarse and not very good to eat.*

Joseph Williams (3)

*...this morning breakfasted on two beaver tails, which I had laid by and forgotten, so we have not yet on this trip lost a meal, as yet...*

Nathaniel Wyeth (4)

The question is, in the midst of all these entries, where do you put the domestic dog? It is found over and over as a food that some groups ate regularly. But it is outside the general bounds of most diets. I put a few entries in the Native Influence chapter, but feel it might fit well here too. The early western traveler had to find for themselves where they thought it fit in on the subject of whether to eat it or not and I will let them tell you in their own words:

*... we found of them without meat, but bought of them a lean dog of which supper and enough for breakfast, so it is rub and go...*

Nathaniel Wyeth (5)

*... traded a knife each for 6 dogs today, used the grease of these dogs to kill the lice on my horses that are nearly covering them...*

Nathaniel Wyeth (6)

*When we returned, my father had prepared lots, that we should draw, to determine who of us should kill one of the dogs. I refused through the fear that the lot might fall on me. These faithful companions of our suffering were so dear to me, that I felt as though I could not allow them to be killed to save my own life; though to save my father, I was aware that it was a duty to allow it to be done. We lay here until the 18th, my father finding the flesh of the dog both sweet, nutritive and strengthening.*

James Pattie (7)

Even the world traveler George Ruxton wrote: *Their meat* [dog] *in appearance and flavor, resembles young pork, but far surpasses it in richness and delicacy of flavor.* (8)

The following show some other unique food sources:

*...and after a delicious meal of roasted sheep ribs, eggs, wheaton cakes and coffee...*

Matthew Field (9)

*Two men whom we met returning home disheartened, told us they were preserved from utter starvation by the lucky shot at a dog [prairie dog], which with a little flour, was their only sustenance for three days.* [The editor's note on prairie dog soup at the bottom of that page says others who tried this declared it "not first class"!]

Matthew Field (10)

*This misfortune prevented our obtaining supplies of meat, and we were consequently reduced to the necessity of living on whatever came to hand. Famished wolves, ravens, magpies, and even raw hide was made tender by two days boiling, were greedily devoured.*

Warren Ferris (11)

The journals give us many angles on what was discussed or written about. Francis Parkman gives us a dream he had while sick on horseback, on a hot spring day near Black Walnut Creek as he writes, slouching on a horse and day dreaming:

*... indulging an epicurean reverie I – dreamed of a cool mountain spring, in a finest country – two bottles of champagne cooling in it and cut glass tumblers, full of the sparkling liquid.* (12)

Zebulon Pike noted in his journal of having such a desire for buffalo marrow that he sent men out to kill a buffalo just for its marrow. (13)

*Brother James dined with us, and supped also on oyster-soup and champain.*
[sp]

Susan Magoffin (14)

Zenas Leonard and some of his company went out hunting for hides to make moccasins, this being November and larger winter moccasins needed to be made for the extra layers on their feet. Along with the hides, they brought back the tongues.

*In the evening the hunters all returned to camp, with the tongues of 93 deer and some of the hides… (15)*

Charles Murray killed a badger but told the men it was a young bear, which satisfied their interest in the kind of meat it was. (He did tell them later.) (16)

*Wagh! Exclaimed LaBonte, we'll have to eat before long and rising, walked into the prairie. He had hardly stepped two paces when passing close to a sage brush, a rattlesnake whizzed a note of warning with its tail. Killbuck grinned, and taking the wiping stick from this rifle barrel, tapped the snake on the head and taking it by the tail, threw it to LaBonte, saying "h'yar meat, any how." The old fellow followed up his success by slaying half-a-dozen more, and brought them in skewered through the head on his wiping stick. A fire was soon kindled…*

George Ruxton (17)

*Our fare consisted of bacon and hard tack – no sugar nor coffee – for three or four days, after which we received a small piece of sheep meat, as we had a drove to last us until we got into the buffalo. While the sheep lasted we had but that alone.*

Charles Larpenteur (18)

[ate] *Raw tallow* (buffalo)

Susan Magoffin (19)

I am now going to single out a western traveler's special foods that she recorded in this section. Susan Magoffin was a young, rich lady recently married to a much older Santa Fe Trail trader. Her diary shows us a very unique set of dinners and they deserve to be included here.

*We had a fine dinner today and I enjoyed it exceedingly, for I had eaten nothing but a little Tea and biscuit since yesterday dinner. It consisted of boiled chicken, soup, rice, and a dessert of wine and gooseberry tart. Such a thing on the plains would be looked upon by those at home as an utter impossibility. But nevertheless, it is true. Jane and I went off as soon as we got here and found enough for a pie. (20)*

*Here we had no wood; there are no trees, and we provided none in the morning so we were obliged to take a dinner of crackers with a little ham fried at the small fire of the wagoneers. It went quite well though with a tin cup of shrub. (21)*

Susan's first dinner in her tent was: ... *as I said after the first supper at my own table consisting of fried ham and eggs, biscuit and a cup of shrub, for I preferred it to tea or café'... (22)*

You will see many of Susan's foods in the different chapters of this book. She was very ready to write about them to her family and we find her notes still interesting today. Besides their uniqueness, I like that she is one of the few women whose journals are still around. So, we get to see a lady's viewpoint on what has been so far mainly a masculine topic.

Another woman who has let us see a lot of special foods is Narcissa Whitman, the wife of missionary Marcus Whitman. She had a tea on the banks of the Laramie River with mountain men, wrote about her foods on the trail to those back home noted a meal that even surprised her:

*...they were just eating breakfast as we rode up soon we were at the table & were treated to fresh Solomon, potatoes, tea, bread and butter. What a variety thought I. (23)*

*... shot at one of the Sioux dogs for chasing my chickens, but unfortunately missed him ...*

Francis Chardon (24)

Francis Chardon may have been keeping the hens around for the eggs, but I am sure they were cooked when they quit laying eggs. But not until the time they were ready to eat it, as a living animal did not have to be preserved to keep its meat from spoiling; it did that for itself! That wasn't the only time the head table had something like chicken found in meals back east. For:

*– caught a chicken by the head in a trap set for rats in the office... (25)*

The chickens must have had free range of the fort and its buildings.

*Between eight and nine o'clock in the evening, I was invited to attend a wedding... the wedding cake was not frosted with sugar nor illustrated with matrimonial devises, after the manner of confectioners in the "settlements," but cake was handed round to the whole party present.*

Edwin Bryant (26)

Washington Irving in his *A Tour of the Prairies* wrote a humorous but disturbing story of how the two Frenchmen in his group had gone in to the brush for a bear but came out with a polecat [skunk]. He wrote:

*When they found, however, that he and Tonish were absolutely bent upon bearing off the carcass as a peculiar dainty, there was a universal expression of disgust...*

[Irving gave orders to get rid of it and they thought he had until:]

*...for after a time, Beatte, who had lagged behind, rode up to the head of the line to resume his station as guide, and I had the vexation to see the carcass of his prize, stripped of its skin, and looking like a fat suckling pig, dangling behind his saddle. I made a solemn vow however, in secret, that our fire should not be disgraced by the cooking of that polecat. (27)*

Washington Irving, later in his journal described a meal he ate at a cabin on the edge of the frontier, which he initially describes as a witches' brew:

*...She was the mistress of house, the spouse of the white man, who was absent. I hailed her as some swart fairy of the wild, that had suddenly conjured up a banquet in the desert; and a banquet was it in good sooth. In a twinkling, she lugged from the fire a huge pot, that might have rivaled one of the famous flesh-pots of Egypt, or the witches' caldron in Macbeth. Placing a brown earthen dish on the floor, she inclined the corpulent caldron on one side and out leaped sundry great morsels of beef, with regiments of turnips tumbling after them, and a rich cascade of broth overflowing the whole. This she handed me with an ivory smile that extended from ear to ear; apologizing for our humble fare, and the humble style in which it was served up. Humble fare! Humble style! Boiled beef and turnips, and an earthen dish to eat them from! To think of apologizing for such a treatment to a half-starved man from the prairies; and then such magnificent slices of bread and butter! Head of Apicius, What a banquet! (28)*

A beaver's meat was a food source for many meals. But as you will see, in some regions these were not to be eaten.

*According to the Carrier custom, a meal was speedily prepared and set before me, consisting of a fat beaver boiled, of which, out of compliment to my host, I slightly partook, the remainder being set aside, and afterwards sent to my tent.*

Peter Skene Ogden (29)

I am not going to convey more than a few words in this chapter on the use of beaver not as a sought after trapping animal, but leave it to be found in previous chapter as a survival food and not as a delicacy.

*...they reported to me that the beaver on this creek had made them sick, probably this was what the matter was with me...*

Nathaniel Wyeth (30)

**Order for sundry articles to be shipped by H. K. Ortley, in the Spring of 1836, per Steam boat addressed to K. Mc Kenzie, Fort Union:**

- 10 gallons best French brandy
- 10 gallons best Hollands gin
- 1 doz 1/2 pint bottles capers
- 1/2 doz qrt bottles best ketchup
- 10 lbs almonds in shell
- 1/2 bushel pearl barley
- 1 box herrings
- A budget of newspapers
- 1 box segars

We find that John Gray liked raisins, and when they dug up their cache, they found a majority of it was wet. These were a luxury at the time, so when the tobacco that was stored with them blended with the raisins, flavoring (he did not chew) it made him sick and was a source of fun by all his companions. He "cast up accounts" was his modest written account of the experience in his journal. (31)

*As we found no buffalo, we had eaten all of the four hundred dried buffalo tongues we had brought...*

E. Willard Smith (32)

*The last one was a cow. For a while she looked on as we flayed a bull, but forfeited her life by her curiosity. She had a calf with her that took to flight. The cow's udder was full of milk. We sucked out the milk and found it refreshing and palatable.*

Fredrick Wislizenus (33)

These unusual foods found their way into the pages of history

*143*

and into this book because of their places within the writer's journals and diaries. Would they be considered as commonplace? No. Historically correct? Yes. These references give us smiles, cringes, and sounds of exclamations. To know of them is what this book is all about. I hope the chapter gives a new "slice" of history.

1.  Osborn Russell, *Journal of a Trapper*, University of Nebraska Press, Lincoln, 1986, page 131.
2.  George Ruxton, *Life in the Far West*, LeRoy Hafen editor, University of Oklahoma Press, Norman, 1985, page 98.
3.  Joseph Williams, *Narrative of a Tour from the State of Indiana to the Oregon Territory in the Years 1841-2*, Ye Galleon Press, Fairfield, 1977, page 32.
4.  Nathaniel Wyeth, *The Journals of Captain Nathaniel J. Wyeth's Expeditions to the Oregon Country, 1831-1836*, Ye Galleon Press, Fairfield, 1997, page 94.
5.  Wyeth, page 95.
6.  Wyeth, page 98.
7.  James Pattie, *The Personal Narrative of James O. Pattie*, University of Nebraska Press, Lincoln, 1984, page 65,
8.  Ruxton, *Life in the Far West*, page 104.
9.  Matthew Field, *Matt Field on the Santa Fe Trail*, John Sunder editor, University of Oklahoma Press, Norman, 1995, page 204.
10. Field, page 286.
11. Warren Ferris, *Life in the Rocky Mountains*, Old West Publishing, Denver, 1983, page 145.
12. Zebulon Pike, *The Southwest Journals of Zebulon Pike*, Stephen Hart & Archer Hulbert editors, University of New Mexico Press, Albuquerque, 2006, page 133.
13. Susan Magoffin, *Down the Santa Fe Trail and into Mexico*, Stella Drumm, editor, Yale University Press, New Haven, 1962, pages 107-8.
14. Zenas Leonard, *Adventures of a Mountain Man*, Milo Quaife editor, University of Nebraska Press, Lincoln, 1978, page 156-7.
15. Charles Murray, *Travels in North America*, William Blackwood and Sons, Edinburgh, 1900, pages 333-4.
16. Ruxton, *Life in the Far West*, page 132.
17. Charles Larpenteur, *Forty Years a Fur Trader on the Upper Missouri*, University of Nebraska Press, Lincoln, 1989, page 17.
18. E. Willard Smith, Colorado Magazine, *With the Fur Traders of Colorado*, July 1950, page 180.
19. Magoffin, pages 36-7.
20. Magoffin, page 7.
21. Magoffin, page 6.

22. Narcissa Whitman, *My Journal,* University of Nebraska Press, Lincoln, 1989, page 39.
23. Francis Chardon, *Chardon's Journal at Fort Clark, 1834-1839*, University of Nebraska Press, Lincoln, 1997, page 49-50.
24. Chardon, page 45.
25. Washington Irving, *A Tour of the Prairies,* University of Oklahoma Press, Norman, 1971, pages 68-9.
26. Edwin Bryant, *Rocky Mountain Adventures*, Ye Galleon Press, Fairfield, 2000, page 91.
27. Irving, page 212.
28. Peter Ogden, *Traits of American Indian Life,* Ye Galleon Press, Fairfield, 1998, page 73.
29. Wyeth, page 93.
30. Chardon, page 383.
31. *Colorado Heritage*, article on John Gray, page 19.
32. E. Willard Smith, page 182.
33. Dr. Fredrick Wislizenus, *A Journey to the Rocky Mountains in the Year 1839*, Ye Galleon Press, Fairfield, 1989, page 55.

# *Fowl*

*Continuing our course, we saw large numbers of prairie-hens, and succeeded in killing several... Their flesh is tender and of superior flavor.*

Rufus Sage (1)

**W**ITH all that has been previously written here on the use of large animals as food; birds or fowl are sections of this bigger theme that are under examined and recognized. While they are to be considered as "small game," they added largely to the western diet. These feathered animals not only gave variety in taste and texture to the appetites of those in the west, it helped round out the hunting opportunities.

Small game, and other easily hunted animals, gave young Native men the opportunity to learn and increase in skill. They were also many times these were the only animals found along the major trails when the larger animals had left because of all the confusion, traffic and noise. So, we should not be surprised to find all kinds of fowl consumed.

*Went out hunting, saw a few buffalo, but killed nothing but a grouse.* (2)

Charles Murray wrote about having buffalo soup with two brace of grouse added. (3)

*Caught one goose which we eat for breakfast...*

Nathaniel Wyeth (4)

*...we saw large flocks of the dusky grouse, (tetrao obscures), a number of which we killed...*

John Townsend (5)

*... killed today a fat goose... killed a duck...*

Nathaniel Wyeth (6)

*...killed four ducks and one swan today, the latter weighed 45 lbs...*

Nathaniel Wyeth (7)

*The ducks and geese, which have swarmed throughout the country during the latter part of autumn, are leaving us, and the swans are arriving in great numbers. These are here, as in all other places, very shy; it is difficult to approach them without cover; but the Indians have adopted a mode of killing them which is very successful; that of drifting upon the flocks at night, in a canoe, in the bow of which, a large fire of pitch pine had been kindled. The swans are dazzled, and apparently stupefied by the bright light, and fall easy victims to the craft of the sportsman.*

John Townsend (8)

*The geese Ducks and Swans are very fat at this season of the year We caught some few Beaver and feasted on Fowls and Eggs...*

Osborne Russell (9)

*...We saw this day great numbers of Prairie Hens, killed several...*

Anthony Glass (10)

*This morning Mr. McLeod remained behind in pursuit of game, and did not come into camp until we had made a long nooning, although we had begun to feel a little concerned about him, yet about 3 o'clock he came into camp loaded with wild ducks, having taken twenty-two.*

Narcissa Whitman (11)

*The large band-tailed pigeon is very abundant near the river, found in flocks of from fifty to sixty, and perching on the dead trees along the maring of the stream. They are feeding upon the buds of the Balsam poplar, are very fat, and excellent eating. In the course of the morning, and without leaving the canoe, I killed enough to supply our people with provision for two days.*

John Townsend (12)

Eggs were very popular on the western frontier, as they were a familiar item in the men's family's diets.

*But one item in our entertainment was indeed a novelty – viz. crow eggs. Almost every tree and bush, skirting the creek at intervals for miles above and below, had been appropriated to the use of countless swarms of crows that populated the surrounding prairies. Sometimes four or five nests of these birds could be seen upon a single tree. On two or three occasions, I obtained six to ten dozen of eggs in the course of an hour. These, whether boiled, roasted, or fried, were found quite an acceptable addition to our bill of daily fare.*

Rufus Sage (13)

Hiram Chittenden in his second volume did say that "The winged portion of the animal creation filled a very small place in the life of the hunter and trapper." (14) Chittenden may have been a great and early chronicler of the west, but he may have had this wrong.

Many of us have turkey around certain annual holidays, so it should not be considered strange to see this to be a part of the diet of the west. The many different animals in this group helped not only to diversify their diets, but adding game birds to their times of eating also provided a good, simple meat that was easy to cook.

1. Rufus Sage, *Rocky Mountain Life*, University of Nebraska Press, Lincoln, 1982, page 43.
2. Nathaniel Wyeth, *The Journals of Captain Nathaniel J. Wyeth's Expeditions to the Oregon Country, 1831-1836*, Ye Galleon Press, Fairfield, 1997, page 54.
3. Sir Charles Murray, *Travels in North America*, William Blackwood and Sons, Edinburgh, 1900, page 335.
4. Wyeth, page 68.
5. John Townsend, *Across the Rockies to the Columbia*, University of Nebraska Press,

**149**

Lincoln, 1978, page 241.
6. Wyeth, page 90.
7. Wyeth, page 93.
8. Townsend, page 226.
9. Osborne Russell, *Journal of a Trapper*, University of Nebraska Press, Lincoln, 1986, page 125.
10. Dan Flores, Anthony Glass, *Journal of an Indian Trader*, Texas A & M, College Station, 1985, page 43.
11. Narcissa Whitman, *My Journal, page 33.*
12. Townsend, page 210.
13. Sage, page 329.
14. Hiram Chittenden, *The American Fur Trade of the Far West*, University of Nebraska Press, Lincoln, 1986, volume two, page 823.

# *Readings on Banquets*

**A**FTER all that has been written here on the small and everyday items of eating, there is one part that has not been mentioned – the feasts. Feasts were special events when cooks went all out and served not only large quantities of whatever they had, but served in the best manner possible.

These times were usually associated with a holiday, a special event or a special gathering. It may have been a winter quarter's meal around the coldest time of the year (on Christmas or New Year's Day) when everyone needed a lift; or a fandango in the southern part of the mountain range; or at a rendezvous when men who had not seen each other since the previous year's gathering had traded their hard earned rewards into money on account. Sometimes these fancy meals were given for just being alive and having survived the elements, the animals and all the situations that were put in front of them while in the west.

The fort ledgers tell us a lot of the tastes and purchases of the individuals. So, reader, be sure to check them out whenever available to you.

Banquets were so special that they were given particular attention in their journals. These feasts were meals not only different than their everyday rations which made these truly times to remember, but as you will see, the manner in which they were served and the atmosphere made these times even better.

Here are a few from my western history library; note what food served, how it was received and what happened to all of it:

> *That night we had a glorious feast. We toasted our distant friends in hot coffee with as much exhilaration as we could have derived from the pure juice of the grape itself. The choicest meats of the cow were subjected to extra culinary touches, and there was not one among us who would have changed his seat upon the grass for a place at the most sumptuous board in Christendom. Here was revelry in its gayest form, smiled upon by heaven through the silver glances of the moon, and not a draught was drained that could return a sting upon the morrow. We laughed, sung, and jested until midnight, when leaving the cow's hump to boil over the fire, we raised a extensive cloud of smoke from burning "buffalo chips" to keep off the mosquitoes, and couched ourselves for the night.*

Matthew Field (1)

> *Here we camped and prepared our dinner, which was by no means to be despised; for be it remembered that we had kept besides a pound or two of tea, coffee, and sugar, a small sack of flour, two or three quarts of beans, and a large piece of fat bacon, or rather bacon fat. Besides these civilized luxuries we had some maize and dried buffalo meat. ... we put into the pot, with three or four quarts of water, a large lump of meat, with some maize and a few beans. When these were boiled they made a very palatable and nutritious soup; in our second course we indulge sinfully a luxury to which we had long been strangers. For we made some small flour-cakes by frying them in bacon fat and finished the repast with a cup of coffee.*

Charles Murray (2)

Banquets were such a big event, that planning went on for days beforehand. A good entry to show this in a Native setting is from Peter Skene Ogden's narrative:

> *...Kanayah came to usher me to his lodge, where the native guests were already assembled. I was placed in a position which commanded a view of the whole assembly, my interpreter being accommodated near me. The other guests were seated on the ground, in rows, back to back, and with the exception of the vacancies preserved between rows, occupied the whole area of the lodge. There were perhaps, two hundred present. Huge piles of dried meats, with vessels of bear's grease and fish-oil, besides quantities of berry-cakes, were stowed up in the vacant places, so as to leave barely room to pass and repass.*

152

Truly, all was done for good reasons and the following quote he wrote on the next page of his book:

*"The Feast of reason and the flow of the soul".* (3)

*I went this day to a great medicine feast of chiefs including all the principle warriors of the Grand Pawnees, the Tapages, the Loups and the Otoe chief. As usual in such cases, the feast consisted of only one kind of food, and the number of wooden bowls and buffalo horn spoons indicated that fifty guests were expected to empty an enormous caldron of maize, which was boiling on a fire before the lodge. No excuses of illness or occupation are ever offered or accepted; and if one guest happens to be absent, the party, however numerous it may be, must patiently await his arrival. On this occasion, we waited an hour and half before the assemblage was complete... As soon as these orations were concluded, twenty-five large wooden bowls of maize were placed before the guests, two spoons being placed in each bowl, the messmates being vis-à-vis, and not side by side. Before a morsel was tasted the first chief set apart one large spoonful, and gave it to the master of the ceremonies, or the officiating medicine man, who made with his scalping knife two small holes in the earth, and having divided the spoonful of maize into two unequal portions, the larger of which was dedicated to the buffalo (subordinate spirit) and smaller to the Great Spirit, he turned to the east, and three times bowed his body, at the same time raising and lowering his hands; then again he turned to his guests, and went through the same ceremonial benediction, after which the work of demolition began.*

Charles Murray (4)

Well-remembered feasts could be large or small. It seems that the thought and intent was what made these dinners so special and not what was served:

*20 very fine salmon, fat buffalo and coffee which would make even the British consider it to be independent.*

Osborne Russell (5)

*The new year was ushered in with feasting and merriment, on dried buffalo meat, and venison, cakes and coffee; which might appear to people constantly accustomed to better fare, rather meager variety for a dinner, not to say a feast. But to us who have constantly in mind the absolute impossibility of procuring better, and the no less positive certainty, that we are often compelled to be satisfied with worse, - the repast was both agreeable and excellent; for think not, that we enjoy, daily, the same luscious luxuries of cake and coffee, that announces the advent of 1834; by no means. Our common meals consist of a piece of boiled venison, with a single addition of a piece of fat from the shoulder of the buffalo...*

Warren Ferris (6)

Feasts were given at the rendezvous by friends and some even sent foods with friends when they left. Having not seen them for a while and knowing they may not see them again for another length of time, they did all they could to show their friendship and keep the camaraderie going well after they separated.

*Before sunset, we were summoned by little Tonish to go to a sumptuous repast. Blankets had been spread on the ground near to the fire, upon which we took our seats. A large dish, or bowl, made from the root of a maple tree, and which we had purchased at the Indian village, was placed on the ground before us, and into it were empted the contents of one of the camp-kettles, consisting of a wild turkey hash, together with slices of bacon and lumps of dough. Beside it was placed another bowl of similar ware, containing an ample supply of fritters. After we had discussed the hash, two wooden spits, on which the ribs of a fat buck were broiling before the fire were removed and planted in the ground before us, with a triumphant air. Having no dishes, we had to proceed in hunter's style, cutting off strips and slices with our hunting knives and dipping them in salt and pepper. To do justice to Tonish's cookery, however, and to the keen sauce of the prairie, never have I tasted venison so delicious. With all this, our beverage was coffee, boiled in a camp-kettle, sweetened with brown sugar, and drunk out of tin cups; and such was the style of our banqueting throughout this expedition, whenever provisions were plenty and as long as flour and coffee and sugar held out.*

Washington Irving (7)

The number of times of feasting in an Indian village during a celebration is told by Albert Pike:

*We passed the remainder of the day and the next one with them* [the Osages], *and were called upon, every hour in the day, to go to some lodge and eat. In the course of the second day and evening, we ate fifteen times, were obligated to do so, or affront them.* (8)

*The day we moved in was a holiday, and in the evening a great feast was given us by Mr. Campbell – Mr. Sublette having left in the keel boat a few days after our arrival, taking ten men with him. It consisted of half a pint of flour to each men, one cup of coffee, one of sugar, and one of molasses to four men. Out of this a becoming feast was made, consisting of thick pancakes, the batter containing not other ingredient than pure Missouri water, greased with buffalo tallow; but as I had had*

154

*nothing of the kind for upward of six months, I thought I had never tasted anything so good in my life and swore I would have plenty of the like if I ever got back to the states.*
Charles Larpenteur (9)

Osborne Russell described a good midwinter feast while in camp with a mixed assemblage of friends:

*... around this sat on clean epishoemores all who claimed kin to the white man (or to use their own expression all that were "gen d'espirit") with their legs crossed in true Turkish style – and now for the dinner. The first dish that came on was a large tin pan 18 inches in diameter rounding full of stewed elk meat. The next dish was similar to the first heaped up with boiled deer meet (or as the whites would call it venison, a term not used in the mountains). The 3rd and 4th dishes were of equal in size to the first containing a boiled flour pudding prepared with dried fruit accompanied by 4 quarts of sauce made of the juice of sour berries and sugar. Then came the cakes followed by about six gallons of strong coffee already sweetened with tin cups and pans to drink out of with large chips or pieces of bark supplying the places of plates. On being ready, the butcher knives were drawn and the eating commenced at the word given by the landlady as all dinners were accompanied with conversation, this was not deficient in that respect. The principle topic which was discussed was the political affairs of the Rocky Mountains, the state of governments among the different tribes, the personal characters of the most distinguished warriors chiefs, etc...Dinner being over, the tobacco pipes were filled and lighted while the [women] and children cleared away the remains of the feast to one side of the lodge where they held a sociable tite a tite over the fragments. (10)*

Francis Chardon's journal gives us record of one memorable meal:

*... last night at ½ past 10 o'clock, we partook of a fine supper prepared by old Charbonneau, consisting of meat pies, bread, fricasseed pheasants, boiled tongues, roast beef – and coffee... the contents of the table was dispatched, some as much as seven cups to nine cups of coffee...as everyone did honor to his plate. (11)*

The feast was eaten in what he calls "a little time" with the help of up to seven to nine cups of coffee each.

Charles Larpenteur had a different kind of Christmas party, all the fare was in "drinkables" and he would drink nothing stronger than tea.

*On this anniversary [Christmas 1838] a great dinner is generally made, but that was never the case here, as it was always taken out in drinkables instead of eatables; and I, who did not drink, had to do without my dinner. (12)*

155

Because Larpenteur was not a drinker, the officers of Fort Union reinstated him in the liquor shop. Probably a wise move, as you would not want anyone who might join the purchasers in times of toasting or drink away some of the profits:

*On new year's day, notwithstanding our horses were nearly all dead, and being fully satisfied that the few that were yet living must die soon, we concluded to have a feast in our best style; for which purpose we made preparation by sending out four of our best hunters, to get a choice piece of meat for the occasion. These men killed ten buffalo, from which we selected one of the fattest humps they could find and brought in, and after roasting it handsomely before the fire, we all seated ourselves upon the ground, encircling, what we there called a splendid repast to dine upon. Feasting sumptuously, cracking a few jokes, taking a few rounds with our rifles, and wishing heartily for some liquor, having none at that place, we spent the day.*

Zenas Leonard (13)

The *Journals of Francis Parkman*, not his *Oregon Trail* book which most are familiar with; but his daily journals which were the basis and notes for the other book, tells of an unusual feast he had while staying with some Indian friends:

*Today, gave them a feast – dog, tea and bread.* (14)

Parkman also wrote of one special dinner at Bent's Fort. Unusual, for the table had a white cloth on it – the first civilized meal he had since leaving Fort Leavenworth the previous May. (15)

The bigger and better forts, like Fort Union, had a table just for the higher ranking men and clerks. Diners weren't allowed to come to the table in shirt sleeves, so Larpenteur had to use a borrowed jacket to be seated. (He had just arrived from another fort where a jacket wasn't required, and he didn't own one.) Two waiters served at the table, which was covered with a white tablecloth, and each plate had two biscuits on it – a rare treat. The clerks sat by grades, which put Larpenteur on the end, since he had just started there. His duties at the fort were to open the gates early in the morning, lock them at night, see that the tool and harness shed were kept in order, plus lend a hand if needed around the stores. He was entrusted with the keys to the fort.

The invitation to eat at a head table was a special thing. A picture of such a table is seen as the opening picture to this chapter, from Bent's Old Fort on the Santa Fe Trail in southeastern Colorado. This table was used for special visitors, and the daily meal times for the upper status of those within the fort. And, the head table could also be used as a way to snub people. You can read between the lines in the following quote one example of this:

>    ...*Kelly is not received at the fort* [Vancouver] *on this account* [stealing some horses from the fort], *as a gentleman, a house is given him and food is sent him from the Gov. table, but he is not suffered to mess here...*
>
>                                      Nathaniel Wyeth (16)

One time at Bent's Fort, I was portraying a clerk employee (since I could read and write), which qualified me to be invited to dine at the head table. Luckily I was second on the list of clerks and not on the end – the last few people to get served have the least to eat!

To come to breakfast with a vest and tailored jacket is not something that I do every day, even at home. And we save our good china and crystal glasses for special occasions, not everyday use; and there are no servants waiting on me these days. But some of the forts, like Bent's, did put on "airs." That situation gave me another unique view of life at a fort. For life in the west did have class and culture in it.

>    *The day of our arrival* [at Fort Hall] *we were invited to a supper at the fort, which would be deemed quite frugal in civilized life, but which, in this wilderness, consisted of the most delicious dishes which we had ever tasted since we started, namely, bread, butter, milk, dried buffalo meat and tea with rum. No Paris meal composed with all a gourmand's art ever tasted better to me, than the luxuries of this feast on the sand slopes of the Snake River.*
>
>                                 Dr. Fredrick Wislizenus (17)

>    *Arriving, we found a pleasant and comfortable camp, and supper nearly ready, and all hands waiting our arrival and anticipating a rich and luxuriant feast of bread, meat and onions, with coffee and plenty of sweetening. And although we dined as should be at the fashionable hour (5 to 7 pm), our bill of fare would be hardly recognized as very high toned or elaborate. The table was a blanket spread upon the ground, and the furniture was a tin plate, an iron spoon and a butcher knife, with a tin cup of coffee. Our bill of fare was soup, followed by meat with bread and honey. And honey on the plate made the bill of fare: soup and honey, meat and honey, bread and honey, coffee and honey and honey for dessert. We were all honeyed, but I think I had the most honey and suffered the most. That night will be ever remembered as one of suffering. But the morning brought comfort, and we proceeded on our journey.*
>
>                                          James Webb (18)

>    ... *About 11 o'clock, met doctor Robinson on a prairie, who informed me that he and Bonney had been absent from the party about two days without killing anything*

*(also without eating) but that over night, they had killed four buffalo, and that he was in search of the men…shortly afterwards, Sparks arrived and informed us he had killed four buffalo cows. Thus from being in a starving condition we had 8 beeves in our camp. We now again found ourselves all assembled together on Christmas Eve and appeared generally to be content, although all the refreshment we had to celebrate that day with, was buffalo meat, without salt, or any other thing whatsoever.*

Zebulon Pike (19)

Feasts were remembered! Not only for the times or events they celebrated, but for the food and friendship in them.

*The mountaineer who has subsisted for months on nothing but fresh meat, would proclaim bread, sugar, and coffee to be high orders of luxury.*

Edwin Bryant (20)

*Notwithstanding the chilliness of the air, I took a bath, and returned to enjoy a fine supper of buffalo meat. "Fleeces", briskets, ribs, tongues, udders, marrow bones, & c. were roasting, boiling, and frying over the merry camp fires.*

Lt. James Abert (21)

After five days of scant or no food, Wislizenus' party heard from the scouts that a mass of Indians were bearing down on them. It turned out, as they pleasantly found, to be a herd of elk instead. They killed one and commented it was much better to live in plenty than being scalped by Blackfeet. Then they commenced:

*Quite systematically we now began to arrange our bill of fare. First soup appeared on the table, then various roasts, and finally sausages stuffed with liver, and marrow bones. Pauses were made between the courses. Our appetite was all that could be desired. Whoever had seen us in civilized life and seen such substantial demonstrations of appetite as we did, would have set us down for a band of hungry wolves or gluttons. But here the whole thing seemed quite natural. (22)*

Food meant life, and food meant it was time to celebrate, to live in the moment and then to go on.

1.   Matthew Field, *Matt Field on the Santa Fe Trail*, John Sunder editor, University of Oklahoma Press, Norman, 1995, page 142.
2.   Charles Murray, *Travels in North America*, William Blackwood and Sons, Edinburgh, 1900, page 279.

3.  Peter Skene Ogden, *Traits of American Indian Life*, Ye Galleon Press, Fairfield, 1998, pages 108-9.

4.  Murray, page 205-7.

5.  Osborne Russell, *Journal of a Trapper*, University of Nebraska Press, Lincoln, 1986, page 97.

6.  Warren Ferris, *Life in the Rocky Mountains*, Old West Publishing, Denver, 1983, pages 310-1.

7.  Washington Irving, *A Tour of the Prairies*, University of Oklahoma Press, Norman, 1971, pages 58-9.

8.  Albert Pike, *Prose, Sketches and Poems*, Texas A & M University Press, College Station, David Webber editor, 1987, page 72.

9.  Charles Larpenteur, *Forty Years a Fur Trader on the Upper Missouri*, University of Nebraska Press, Lincoln, 1989, pages 42-3.

10. Russell, pages 114 - 6.

11. Francis Chardon, *Chardon's Journal at Fort Clark, 1834-1839*, University of Nebraska Press, Lincoln, 1997, page 18.

12. Larpenteur, page 134.

13. Zenas Leonard, *Adventures of a Mountain Man*, Milo Quaife editor, University of Nebraska Press, Lincoln, 1978, pages 20-1.

14. Francis Parkman, *The Journals of Francis Parkman*, Harper and Brothers, New York, 1947 (two volumes), page 457.

15. Parkman, page 636.

16. Nathaniel Wyeth, *The Journals of Captain Nathaniel J. Wyeth's Expeditions to the Oregon Country, 1831-1836*, Ye Galleon Press, Fairfield, 1997, page 99.

17. Dr. Fredrick Wislizenus, *A Journey to the Rocky Mountains in the Year 1839*, Ye Galleon Press, Fairfield, 1989, page 107.

18. James Josiah Webb, *Adventures in the Santa Fe Trade 1844-1847*, Ralph Bieber editor, University of Nebraska, Lincoln, 1995, pages 168-9.

19. Zebulon Pike, *The Southwest Journals of Zebulon Pike*, Stephen Hart & Archer Hulbert editors, University of New Mexico Press, Albuquerque, 2006, page 156.

20. Edwin Bryant, *Rocky Mountain Adventures*, Ye Galleon Press, Fairfield, 2000, page 113.

21. Lt. James Abert, *Expedition to the Southwest*, University of Nebraska Press, Lincoln, 1999, page 96.

22. Wislizenus, pages 134-5.

# *Conclusion*

**T**HE foods of the west were as unique as each of the characters who ate them. As you have seen, a recipe or cook book was not needed for the large majority of the meals; you had something in hand and needed to cook it with what you had around you. It was as plain and simple as that. Making it interesting after having the same thing over and over was the catch. These individuals did recognize and appreciate the different parts of animals much more than we do today. For many sections of the animals were cooked differently than we think and the textures and tastes were also different, even within the same animal. Anyone who does not think this is correct, should think of the differences between a buffalo's tongue, its chewy liver and the animal's marbled hump.

As you can see from these pages, many different animals, plants, fruits and fish were consumed in everyday life. Regional and ethnic influences determined the average table fare, along with what was in season or within range of hunting and gathering.

Sometimes this part of the west is found recorded in a humorous style in the journals:

*Here we caught plenty of fish and found a bee tree from which we furnished ourselves with honey. One of our company, named Ferguson, was bitten by a rattlesnake. We gave him rattlesnake master and a quart of whiskey, which seemed to have little or no effect as to inebriation but soon relieved the pain of the bite and the man rapidly recovered.*

Jacob Robinson (1)

Here we see honey, fish and whiskey- three of the chapter topics of this book in one journal entry; a real bonanza of interesting foods in one event.

I always find food cooked outdoors to taste better than if done over an electric stovetop, by a gas stove or in a microwave oven. I don't know if it is the setting, the people around when this is going on or just that the food soaks up all that is going on around it and it enhances the taste.

I hope you have found the subject of the cuisine in the early west to be well worth the effort. The information found in these pages will change how I think of meal times and their application to my outings. I guess this is like every other kind of knowledge – not much good unless it is applied to our lives. The stores, the hauling, preparation and preserving of them and variety of western foods, all add up to a topic that was found on every page of each of the old journals, diaries and autobiographies, yet largely overlooked. How the edible situation went affected how the day and camp was.

Food can make history come alive, like no other item can. Sometimes the subject is only found by the reader between the lines. But all this makes the west even more interesting and exciting. I will end this with a journal entry of William Anderson:

*Here I am, at a beautiful spring, my skewer in the ground at a hot fire of buffalo dung, a set of good sweet hump-ribs roasting before me, legs crossed, knife drawn and mouth watering, waiting for the attack. At just such a time I have forgotten home, Indians, everything but my ribs and my sweetheart, and but for hope association*

*I think she, too, would have been put behind me. These clear mountain springs are charming places. They do so sweetly wash down a savory meal of buffalo meat. And is such a meal really good? What a question to a hungry man* (2)

So, please forgive me. I suddenly find myself hungry – for some reason – and must end this. A glowing fire is calling me.

1. Jacob Robinson, *Journal of the Santa Fe Expedition*, Narrative Press, Santa Barbara, 2001, page 2.
2. William Anderson, *The Rocky Mountain Journals of William Marshall Anderson*, University of Nebraska Press, Lincoln, 1987, page 117.

# Bibliography

Lt. James Abert, *Expedition to the Southwest*, University of Nebraska Press, Lincoln, 1999.

David Adams, *The David Adam's Journals*, Charles Hanson, Jr. editor, Museum of the Fur Trade, Chadron, 1994.

William Anderson, *The Rocky Mountain Journals of William Marshall Anderson*, University of Nebraska Press, Lincoln, 1987.

John Woodhouse Audubon, *Audubon's Western Journal*, University of Arizona Press, Tucson, 1905.

Alexander Barclay, *Mountain Man*, George Hammond, Old West Publishing, Denver, Colorado, 1976.

Michael Bell, *Braves and Buffalo*, University of Toronto Press, 1973.

Maxine Benson, *From Pittsburg to the Rocky Mountains, Major Stephen Long's Expedition 1819-1820*, Fulcrum Books, Golden, Colorado, 1988.

Henry Brewer, *The Journal of Henry Brewer*, Richard Seiber editor, Ye Galleon Press, Fairfield, 1986.

George Brewerton, *Overland with Kit Carson*, University of Nebraska, Lincoln, 1993.

Diane Brotemarkle, *Fort St. Vrain*, self published, Boulder, 2001.

David Brown *Three Years in the Rocky Mountains*, Ye Galleon Press, Fairfield, 1982.

Edwin Bryant, *Rocky Mountain Adventures*, Ye Galleon Press, Fairfield, 2000.

Robert Campbell, *A Narrative of Colonel Robert Campbell's, Experiences in the Rocky Mountain Fur Trade from 1825-1835*, Drew Hollway, editor, Ye Galleon Press, Fairfield, Washington, 1999.

George Catlin, *Letters and Notes on the North American* Indians, JG Press, North Dighton, 1995.

Francis Chardon, *Chardon's Journal at Fort Clark, 1834-1839*, University of Nebraska Press, Lincoln, 1997.

Hiram Chittenden, *The American Fur Trade of the Far West*, University of Nebraska Press, Lincoln, 1986 (two volumes).

James Clyman, *Journal of a Mountain* Man, Mountain Press Publishing, Missoula, 1984.

Richard Henry Dana, *Two Years before the Mast*, Signet Classic, New York, 2000.

Clifford Drury, *On to Oregon*, University of Nebraska Press, Lincoln, 1998.

Francis Ermatinger, *The Fur Trade Letters of Francis Ermatinger*, Lois Halliday

McDonald, Arthur Clark Company, Glendale, 1980.

William Fairholme, *Journal of an Expedition to the Grand Prairies of the Missouri*, Arthur Clark, Spokane, 1996.

Thomas Farnum, *Travels in the Great Western Prairies, the Anahuac and Rocky Mountains and in the Oregon Territory*, private reprint by Don Erickson and Bob Elsloo, 2007.

Warren Ferris, *Life in the Rocky Mountains*, Old West Publishing, Denver, 1983.

Matthew Field, *Matt Field on the Santa Fe Trail*, John Sunder editor, University of Oklahoma Press, Norman, 1995.

Dan Flores, *Journal of an Indian Trader*, Texas A & M, College Station, 1985.

Jacob Fowler, *The Journal of Jacob Fowler*, Elliot Coues, editor, Ross & Haines, Inc., Minneapolis, 1965.

Lewis Garrard, *Wah-to-yah and the Taos Trail*, University of Oklahoma Press, Norman, 1957.

Josiah Gregg, *Commerce of the Prairies*, Milo Milton Quaife, editor, University of Nebraska Press, Lincoln, 1967.

Kate Gregg, *The Road to Santa Fe, the Journal and Diaries of George Champlin Sibley*, University of New Mexico Press, Albuquerque, 1952.

LeRoy Hafen, *The Fur Trade of the Far West*, Spokane, Arthur Clark Company, ten volumes, 2001.

George Hammond, *Alexander Barclay, Mountain Man*, Old West Publishing Company, Denver, 1976.

Lansing Hasting, *The Emigrant's Guide*, Applewood books, Bedford, no date,

James Hobbs, *Wild Life in the Far West*, Rio Grande Press, Glorieta, 1969.

Kenneth Holmes, *Covered Wagon Women*, (volume one), University of Nebraska Press, Lincoln, 1983.

Kenneth Holmes, *Ewing Young*, Abinfords and Mort Publishing, Portland, Oregon, 1967.

John Treat Irving, *Indian Sketches*, University of Oklahoma Press, Norman, 1955.

Washington Irving, *A Tour of the Prairies*, University of Oklahoma Press, Norman, 1971.

Paul Kane, *Wanderings of an* Artist, Charles Tuttle Company, Rutland, 1968.

Thomas James, *Three Years Among the Indians and Mexicans*, Milo Quaife editor, Citadel Press, New York, 1966.

Rudolph Kurz, *On the Upper Missouri*, Carla Kelly, editor, University of Oklahoma Press, Norman, 2005.

Charles Larpenteur, *Forty Years a Fur Trader on the Upper Missouri*, University of Nebraska Press, Lincoln, 1989.

Reginald Laubin, The Indian Tipi, Stanley Vestal, editor, University of Oklahoma Press, Norman, 1977.

Zenas Leonard, *Adventures of a Mountain Man*, Milo Quaife editor, University of Nebraska Press, 1978.

Susan Magoffin, *Down the Santa Fe Trail and into Mexico*, Stella Drumm, editor, Yale University Press, New Haven, 1962.

Randolph Marcy, *The Prairie Traveler*, Applewood Books, Bedford, 1993,

Prince Maximilian, *People of the First Man*, Davis Thomas & Karin Ronnefeldt, editors, Promontory Press, New York, 1982.

David Meriwether, *My Life in the Mountains and on the Plains*, University of Oklahoma Press, Norman, 1965.

Mike Moore, *Heroes to Me*, Historical Enterprises, Macon, Georgia, 2003.

Dale Morgan, *The West of William H. Ashley*, Old West Publishing Company, Denver, Colorado, 1964.

Charles Murray, *Travels in North America*, William Blackwood and Sons, Edinburgh, 1900.

Joseph Nicollet, *Joseph N. Nicollet on the Plains and Prairies*, Edmund and Martha Bray editors, Minnesota Historical Society, St. Paul, 1993.

Peter Skene Ogden, *Traits of American Indian Life*, Ye Galleon Press, Fairfield, 1998.

Francis Parkman, *The Journals of Francis Parkman*, Harper and Brothers, New York, 1947, (two volumes).

James Pattie, *The Personal Narrative of James O. Pattie*, University of Nebraska Press, Lincoln, 1984.

Jerome Peltier, *Black Harris*, self published, Spokane, 1986.

Albert Pike, *Prose, Sketches and Poems*, Texas A & M University Press, College Station, David Webber editor, 1987.

Zebulon Pike, *The Southwest Journals of Zebulon Pike*, Stephen Hart & Archer Hulbert editors, University of New Mexico Press, Albuquerque, 2006.

Nicholas Point, Wilderness *Kingdom*, Loyola Press, Chicago, 1967.

Jacob S. Robinson, *The Journal of the Santa Fe Expedition*, Narrative Press, Santa Barbara, 2001.

Alexander Ross, *Adventures of the First Settlers on the Oregon or Colombia River, 1810-1813*, University of Nebraska Press, Lincoln, 1986.

Osborne Russell, *Journal of a Trapper*, University of Nebraska Press, 1986.

Terry Russell, *Messages from the President on the State of the Fur Trade*, 1824-1832, Ye Galleon Press, 1985.

George Ruxton, *Ruxton of the Rockies*, LeRoy Hafen, editor, University of Oklahoma Press, Norman, 1982.

George Ruxton, *Life in the Far West*, LeRoy Hafen, editor, University of Oklahoma Press, Norman, 1985.

Rufus Sage, *Rocky Mountain Life*, University of Nebraska Press, Lincoln, 1982.

George Sibley, *The Road to Santa Fe*, Kate Gregg editor, University of New

Mexico Press, Albuquerque, 1968.

Eliza Smith, *The Compleat Housewife*, published in 1748, Studio Editions facsimile edition.

Jedediah Smith, *a Southwest Expedition of Jedediah Smith*, University of Nebraska Press, Lincoln, 1989.

Sir William Drummond Stewart, *Edward Warren*, Mountain Press, Missoula, 1986.

David Thompson, *Columbia Journals*, Barbara Belyea, editor, University of Washington Press, Seattle, 1994.

John Kirk Townsend, *Across the Rockies to the Columbia*, University of Nebraska Press, Lincoln, 1978.

James Josiah Webb, Adventures *in the Santa Fe Trade 1844-1847*, Ralph Bieber editor, University of Nebraska, Lincoln, 1995.

David Webber, *Taos Trappers*, University of Oklahoma, Norman, 1968.

Narcissa Whitman, *My Journal*, University of Nebraska Press, Lincoln, 1989..

Joseph Williams, *Narrative of a Tour from the State of Indiana to the Oregon Territory in the Years 1841-2*, Ye Galleon Press, Fairfield, 1977.

Dr. Fredrick Wislizenus, *A Journey to the Rocky Mountains in the Year 1839*, Ye Galleon Press, Fairfield, 1989.

Nathaniel Wyeth, *The Journals of Captain Nathaniel J. Wyeth's Expeditions to the Oregon Country, 1831-1836*, Ye Galleon Press, Fairfield, 1997.

**Magazine articles used:**

Colorado Heritage, by John Gray

E. Willard Smith, Colorado Magazine, Colorado Historical Society July 1950.

Phillip Covington, *Colorado Magazine,* Colorado Historical Society.

# Index

# Index of Pictures

*All pictures take by author, unless noted.*

# *Special Thanks*

A special thanks to Bill Gwaltney. One day he and I were sitting around looking for something to do, and we came up with this as topic to think about.

Bill, I have said many times that you have given one of the most informative and educational hands on demonstrations. I will never forget sitting on the Arkansas River in the cottonwoods just within gun shot of Bent's Fort and experiencing your class on "drinks of the frontier." What a great time.

Your knowledge and help with this project does not go unnoticed.
Thanks, friend!

# Other books written by Mike Moore

Heroes to Me (2003)
The Rocky Mountain Album (2004)
Life in the Early West (2006)
A View to the West (2008)
2011 Masonic Almanac (2010)
2012 Masonic Almanac (2011)
2013 Masonic Almanac (2012)

Mike has also written over 180 articles over the twenty years as an author, staff writer and lecturer. Many of his individual topics can be seen in past issues of different history magazines. He has appeared on the History Channel, helping with educational aspects of the early intermountain west or finding and learning about hard to reach and unheard of historic sites.